Navigating the Cybersecurity Career Path

Navigating the Cybersecurity Career Path

Helen E. Patton

WILEY

Published by John Wiley & Sons, Inc., Hoboken, New Jersey.
Published simultaneously in Canada.

978-1-119-83342-0
978-1-119-83367-3 (ebk.)
978-1-119-83343-7 (ebk.)

For general information on our other products and services or for technical support, please contact our Customer Care Department within the United States at (800) 762-2974, outside the United States at (317) 572-3993 or fax (317) 572-4002.

Wiley also publishes its books in a variety of electronic formats. Some content that appears in print may not be available in electronic formats. For more information about Wiley products, visit our web site at www.wiley.com.

Library of Congress Control Number: 2021946526

Cover Image: © hkeita/Getty
Cover Design: Wiley

SKY10030910_102721

For Darren and Bear

Contents at a Glance

Foreword: Navigating the Cybersecurity Career Path *xv*
Introduction *xvii*

Part I Arriving in Security **1**

Chapter 1 How Do You Become a Security Professional? 3

Chapter 2 Why Security? 19

Chapter 3 Where Can I Begin? 29

Chapter 4 What Training Should I Take? 41

Chapter 5 What Skills Should I Have? 53

Chapter 6 Is My Résumé Okay? 67

Chapter 7 Trying with Little Success? 81

Part II Thriving in Security **93**

Chapter 8 How Do I Keep Up? 97

Chapter 9 How Can I Manage Security Stress? 107

Chapter 10 How Can I Succeed as a Minority? 119

Chapter 11 How Can I Progress? 129

Chapter 12 Should I Manage People? 143

Chapter 13 How Can I Deal with Impostor Syndrome? 153

Chapter 14 How Can I Know If It's Time to Move On? 163

Part III Leading Security **175**

Chapter 15 Where Do I Start? 179

Chapter 16 How Do I Manage Security Strategically? 187

Chapter 17 How Do I Build a Team? 201

Chapter 18 How Do I Write a Job Posting? 217

Chapter 19 How Do I Encourage Diversity? 227

Chapter 20 How Do I Manage Up? 241

Chapter 21 How Do I Fund My Program? 253

Chapter 22 How Do I Talk About My Security Program? 263

Chapter 23 What Is My Legacy? 275

Epilogue *285*

Appendix: Resources *287*

About the Author *291*

Acknowledgments *293*

Index *295*

Contents

Foreword: Navigating the Cybersecurity Career Path *xv*

Introduction *xvii*

Part I Arriving in Security **1**

Chapter 1 How Do You Become a Security Professional? 3

Create Your Story 8

So, You Want to Work in Security 13

What's Next? 16

Chapter 2 Why Security? 19

What Kind of People Do Security? 21

What Is Your Why? 24

What's Next? 28

Chapter 3 Where Can I Begin? 29

What Does It Mean to Be a Security Professional? 32

How Can You Make Sense of It All? 35

What's Next? 39

Chapter 4 What Training Should I Take? 41

For the Traditional Student 43

For the Nontraditional Student 44

For the Full-Time Nonsecurity Worker 45

Other Things to Consider 46
What's Next? 51

Chapter 5 What Skills Should I Have? 53
The Entry Point — Technology 55
Professional Skills 59
What's Next? 66

Chapter 6 Is My Résumé Okay? 67
Linking the Résumé to the Job Posting 70
Elements of a Résumé 71
Digital Presence 77
References 78
Cover Letters 79
What's Next? 80

Chapter 7 Trying with Little Success? 81
Physical Location 85
Your Company 85
Get Specific 86
Know Your Market 88
Assess Your Efforts So Far 89
But I'm Doing All Those Things! 91
What's Next? 92

Part II Thriving in Security 93

Chapter 8 How Do I Keep Up? 97
Fitting It Into Your Schedule 99
Ad Hoc and Planned Learning 102
Take a Mini-Sabbatical 103
Where Do I Find the Information? 103
What's Next? 105

Chapter 9 How Can I Manage Security Stress? 107
The Stress of Working in Security 109
Managing Security Stress 113
What's Next? 118

Chapter 10 How Can I Succeed as a Minority? 119
Making Security Work for You 124
What's Next? 128

Chapter 11 How Can I Progress? 129
The Security Journey 131
The Opportunist 132
The Intentional Career Seeker 136
How to Get Promoted 139
What's Next? 141

Chapter 12 Should I Manage People? 143
Leadership and Management 145
Preparing for Your Next Role 150
What's Next? 152

Chapter 13 How Can I Deal with Impostor Syndrome? 153
Fact-Check Your Inner Monologue 157
Know Competence and Incompetence 158
Know When to Ask for Help 159
Keep Learning and Know When Enough Is Enough 160
Keep Track of Your Successes 161
What's Next? 162

Chapter 14 How Can I Know If It's Time to Move On? 163
Are You Happy Where You Are? 165
Have You Done All You Wanted to Do? 166
Have You Learned All You Wanted? 167
What Are Your Long-Term Goals? 168
Are You Being Pigeonholed? 169
Do You Fit Into the Culture? 170
Job Hopping 171
Are the Other Options Better than Your Current Job? 172
What's Next? 173

Part III Leading Security 175

Chapter 15 Where Do I Start? 179

What's on Fire? 180
What Is Your Timeline to Act? 181
Who Are Your Partners? 182
Find the Strengths and Note the Weaknesses 183
Draw the Business Risk Picture 184
Do You Have a Mandate? 185
What's Next? 186

Chapter 16 How Do I Manage Security Strategically? 187

Consider Your Industry 190
Know Your Business Priorities 191
Be Pragmatic 193
Address Stakeholder Pain Points 194
Threats and Vulnerabilities 195
Rinse and Repeat 197
Putting It Together 198
What's Next? 200

Chapter 17 How Do I Build a Team? 201

It Is About the How 203
Things to Consider 207
Identify Important Things 209
Identify Areas of Weakness 211
Discontinuing a Function 212
Building New Functions 213
What's Next? 215

Chapter 18 How Do I Write a Job Posting? 217

The Challenge of Job Postings 220
What's Next? 225

Chapter 19 How Do I Encourage Diversity? 227
Start with Numbers 229
Understand Your Cultural Issues 230
Attracting Diverse Talent 232
Writing the Job Description and Posting 234
The Interviewing Process 235
Retaining Diverse Talent 236
Promotions and Career Development 237
Leaving the Team 239
What's Next? 239

Chapter 20 How Do I Manage Up? 241
Who Are Senior Stakeholders? 242
Help Them Understand Security 246
When Things Go Wrong 250
What's Next? 251

Chapter 21 How Do I Fund My Program? 253
Funding a Team 255
Funding a Program 256
The Big Ask 260
What's Next? 261

Chapter 22 How Do I Talk About My Security Program? 263
What Story Should I Tell? 264
Telling Stories 271
What's Next? 273

Chapter 23 What Is My Legacy? 275
Making an Impact on the Industry 277
Making an Impact on Your Company 281
What's Next? 283

Epilogue 285

Appendix: Resources 287

About the Author 291

Acknowledgments 293

Index 295

Foreword: Navigating the Cybersecurity Career Path

"Well, how did I get here?" David Byrne's plaintive question from the Talking Heads song "Once In a Lifetime" is a constant refrain for most of the cybersecurity professionals I know, and the longer they've been in the industry, the more interesting and varied the answers. The sheer intellectual challenge of trying to protect new technologies from misuse, abuse, and destruction draws people from all walks of life: biology, oceanography, physics, liberal arts, theology, and even Chinese philosophy. The number of "tribes" in cybersecurity is also infinite, from the stereotypical hooded hacker to the medical device researcher, military strategist, and human factors designer. This presents a wealth of possibilities to someone who wants to enter the cybersecurity field but makes it even harder to figure out what path to take.

As a liberal arts dropout with ADHD, I find the dizzying maze of career paths suits me. I combined my on-the-job technical knowledge with my foreign language skills and ended up running regional security for a Swiss bank in Europe, and then I went home to Texas to do it again for the state government (yes, Texan cyber is its own dialect). I spent five years as an industry analyst, talking with hundreds of security vendors, before helping to stand up the Retail and Hospitality Intelligence Sharing and Analysis Center. Today I lead a team of former chief information security officers and apply all that experience to help guide security strategy at Cisco, the world's largest security company as well as a networking giant. I have no idea what I might do next in my career; none of it was planned, and every day brings something new for me to figure out.

But for those of you who feel anxious about working your way into your first cybersecurity job, or who are ready to move on to the next step but can't decide what that should be, Helen Patton is the mentor you need. *Navigating the Cybersecurity Career Path* reads like a couple of hours and a hot beverage with her, and if only I'd had either the mentorship or the written version 25 years ago, I might have made different choices in my career. I certainly would have made fewer mistakes. You don't have to be new to the field to get rich insights from her: no matter where you are or what you're trying to master, Helen has wise words from hard-earned experience on how to decide whether security management is right for you, how to build your first cybersecurity program, or even whether it's time to move on from your current position.

Although Helen currently reports to me at work, in a slightly alternate universe I would probably report to her, and I hope I get to do so in the future. The cybersecurity field is so dynamic and new that you should never pass up a chance to learn from a brilliant colleague, and with this book you have that chance in your hands. Seize it, and secure your future!

Wendy Nather
Head of Advisory CISOs, Cisco

Introduction

Every week, I get a call from someone I don't know (or barely know) asking for a meeting so they can get to know me and ask me questions about working in security. Often, the person is thinking about working in security and needs help figuring out where to start. Just as often, the person already works in security and is wrestling with some challenge they can't solve on their own and wants some guidance. Sometimes, the person has taken on a new leadership or management role, and they are overwhelmed with the responsibility and don't know where to start.

They ask questions like these:

- How did you get into security?
- What would you recommend I do about this problem?
- How do you balance your work and home life?

I ask questions like these:

- Where do you work now?
- What do you want the outcome to be?
- Have you read this book/blog/podcast?

Being a mentor, coach, and sounding board is one of my favorite things to do. I love the community of people who work in this profession, and I love helping people navigate their way into and through it. I typically meet with a couple of people each month. Sometimes, meeting a new person results in an ongoing mentoring relationship, with a regular meeting cadence and a specific issue we explore. Sometimes, it results in no further meetings, but we do form a common connection, where I learn more about them. Usually, I also take something away from our meeting, too. I learn something that helps me remember something I had forgotten or something that helps me in my current role. We start a thread that can be picked up later if either of us needs it.

Over the years, I have enjoyed meeting people who are in different stages of their professional journeys. They usually fall into one of three categories:

- Someone who is trying to get into security as their first career or who is coming from another profession
- Someone who is already in security and navigating some mid-career challenges
- Someone who is in a security leadership role and is working out how to be effective

The first meeting is concerned with learning about the other person, making an intellectual and emotional connection, and recognizing where help is needed and where help can be given. Sometimes, I find that I'm the one who needs help, and we realize that regardless of our respective backgrounds or how long each of us has been working, we each have something worth sharing.

I've been in the security industry for a couple of decades, and my own journey has been one of trial and error, good luck, and hard work. I'm now in a place where I have enough experience to provide insight into most questions people ask. I'm also connected to enough really amazing people who will know an answer to a question if I don't. Between blogging, public speaking, and working as a chief information security officer (CISO), I continue to learn about how to be happy and successful in security. I also know that I don't have all the answers and that the path people are on today cannot be the same path I walked. And I have learned that I have a lot to learn!

The security industry is unique. Although the issues have been around for a long time, the industry itself is young compared to other professions. There aren't many established organizational structures or career ladders. The way of doing security varies heavily between different industries and companies. There are no generally accepted security principles or professional standards. Not yet. This makes the security field hard to navigate.

People ask similar questions at each stage of their careers. We all struggle with the same things as we move through this profession. The industry, the company, the manager they work for might be different, but the issues and concerns are common. Often, the person knows what to do or how to find answers, but they need to bounce their ideas off someone else first. They find me or someone like me who can offer wisdom and objectivity. We know enough about the industry to help, but we aren't wrapped up in the day-to-day issues. It helps them confirm that they're not dealing with a unique situation, that someone else has been in the same trench, and that help is available. I play the role of listener, coach, and cheerleader. It is tremendously satisfying.

Meeting people one-on-one doesn't scale very well. As my colleagues and I work hard to attract new people to our industry and help people thrive and lead, the number of people who need help navigating their security careers grows. I wrote this book about the common questions I am asked and to make a widely available resource for people who can't meet me in person. I hope this will also help mentors like me, who can't address all the questions all the time and would like to direct people to a useful resource.

I considered creating three different books (getting into security, living in security, and leading security). As I thought more about it, I realized that our careers aren't linear. Sometimes, we are just starting out in a leadership role. Sometimes, we are decades into one security job, but we are thinking of jumping into a new role and need to work out how to break into security all over again. Sometimes, the challenges we have as a mid-career professional are the same ones we have as leaders. I realized that a person might want to read ahead or revisit certain topics, so keeping them all together would make for one easy reference.

I assume that if you want to work in security (or you already do), then your target company is large enough to support dedicated security resources. This can mean a start-up that is moving into the next phase of growth and needs its first-ever security professional, or it could be a large enterprise with many security teams under one security leader. In any case, my advice applies to people in companies who have some organizational culture and structure.

The topics in each chapter can be read from the perspective of the job seeker, the job holder, or the manager — and sometimes all at once. For example, the chapters about writing a résumé, creating a job posting, and building a diverse team are all related, and there is something in each of these chapters for everyone. I encourage you to look at your questions from "the other side." If you're a job seeker, read the manager chapters to see what they're thinking. If you're a manager, consider the perspective of the job hunter. Security professionals are at their best when they think broadly about a problem. Take the same approach here and explore your questions from all sides.

In each chapter, I begin with a summary section. The summary allows you to quickly find the information you need and to pull out the key themes and resources. You will notice that many themes carry over from chapter to chapter. For the entire book and your entire career, this means you should know yourself, network, stay curious, and communicate well (and often!).

Summary

- **Know yourself:** Know why you are in security. Know what energizes you, how you like to work and communicate, and what motivates you. Constantly seek out jobs and experiences that play to these qualities. Be authentic.
- **Network:** Make building your network a core piece of "being at work," and make room to interact with people in person and online. Use your network for information, for support, and to give back to the community. I can't state how important this is. Being only a person away from almost any answer in cybersecurity is a huge advantage.
- **Stay curious:** There will never be a time where you can "set it and forget it." Keep learning about technology, people, and yourself, and apply that learning as fast as you can.
- **Communicate well and often:** Know how to talk about security and your role in it with as many people as possible. Be clear in your written and spoken communications and be prepared to share widely. Build your relationships with your stories.

You can read this book by just reading the chapters that answer your immediate questions, though advice in one chapter might apply to others, so I would encourage you to read it all. It's helpful to know the answers to questions you have now and also questions you might have in the future. People will be coming to you with these questions at some point, so this is for the future mentor you will be, too. "Be prepared" is a great motto for anyone in security to follow.

You will notice that not many of the questions you will be asked are technology questions. Yes, security is a technology-focused discipline. Yes, you need to have some level of technical expertise to have a role in security. But how to "do" technology is rarely the question people ask mentors about. More often, the questions are about finding resources and navigating organizational structures, personalities, and politics. Security-specific issues must be considered, and I discuss these as they arise, but the presence of technology is a starting point, not the main point.

I didn't write the book in a day — or even a year. When I revisited each chapter during the editing process, I realized that my own ideas about a topic changed with time. As I write this introduction, we are in the middle of the COVID pandemic, and ideas of remote work, inclusion and equity, and career opportunities are changing. I have tried to make my thoughts as time-agnostic as possible and have provided resources that you can use for more information. If any question is interesting to you, I encourage you to do further research. I'm sure there will be more and newer information waiting out there for you to find. I often post questions about security careers and philosophies on LinkedIn (LinkedIn.com/in/helenpatton) or Twitter (@cisoHelen). The answers from the security community are always interesting, often frustrating, and usually thoughtful. I continue to crowdsource my own learning using social media, and you're welcome to follow along. I wish I could include everything

I learn in each chapter! Instead, I hope I give you a way of thinking about a question that leads to a solution you can apply to your own path.

So, grab the beverage of your choice and join me as I consider these common questions. There are no right answers, only better questions, which can lead you to solutions. Let's begin.

PART I

Arriving in Security

This part is for people who are thinking about working in security or trying to assist a job seeker. Each chapter in this section covers the questions job seekers most often ask.

Chapter 1, "How Do You Become a Security Professional?"
We explore ways for you to determine what kind of security job you want and how to find paths to that kind of work.

Chapter 2, "Why Security?"
Here, we think about why security is important to you and what strengths and skills you bring to a security role.

Chapter 3, "Where Can I Begin?"

We learn more about the different kinds of security roles and consider how your own background applies.

Chapter 4, "What Training Should I Take?"

We discuss traditional and nontraditional learning paths, including degrees, boot camps, certifications, and internships.

Chapter 5, "What Skills Should I Have?"

Security professionals need technical skills. They also need professional skills like communications, emotional intelligence, and organization.

Chapter 6, "Is My Résumé OK?"

This is a primer on what to include in a résumé and cover letter.

Chapter 7, "Trying With Little Success?"

When you're not landing the job you want, we discuss how to troubleshoot your process.

CHAPTER

1

How Do You Become a Security Professional?

Summary

How do you write your own security story?

- **Know your why:** Understand your strengths and likes and values, and be able to articulate why security aligns with those things.
- **Stay open to opportunity:** The security path will be unexpected. Be prepared to take on projects and roles that you might not have originally anticipated. Be open

to roles that might not be an exact match for your expectations or skillset.

- **You don't need to be perfect:** No one will have all the skills at exactly the right time. Consider taking opportunities as a way of learning new things.
- **Stay curious:** To be successful in security, there will always be something new to learn. Actively seek knowledge and apply it quickly. Stay in roles long enough to learn all you need to know, and don't skip from role to role too quickly.
- **Find out how others made it into security:** Your path will be different; take what works for you and leave the rest.
- **Network:** Finding the next role will be easier if you have a wide range of people helping you.

Asking someone how they got to their current security job is a great way to break the ice and build a relationship. It is interesting to know how someone made their way through the maze of security functions, corporate politics, and human error to land in their current role. The thing to remember is that a person's story is just that — *their* story — and is not something that you can copy for yourself. My story started in Australia in the late 1980s. I started doing information technology (IT) in the United States in the early 1990s. Think about that for a second: different country, different culture, and different technology. Knowing how I got from being an Australian high school student to being a chief information security officer (CISO) in Columbus, Ohio, makes for an interesting story, but knowing the details of my journey leaves little to take away for someone who is just starting out.

So, should you ask how someone made it into security and how they continue on their security path? Yes. Absolutely. But don't just ask one person; ask anyone you get to meet in security. And don't just ask how they got to be a [fill-in-the-blank] security person. Conduct your own research and look for themes of success. Ask them how they started and how they got to where they are now. What is common about the people who are in roles you want? How do they think? What training did they do? Did they have a mentor to help them? Were they able to stay in one geographic place, or did they have to move around a lot? What kind of family structure did they have? Did they get help, and if so, where did they get that help? And what kind of help did they get?

If you don't know many security people (yet), you might want to read *Tribe of Hackers: Cybersecurity Advice from the Best Hackers in the World* by Marcus J. Carey and Jennifer Jin. This book contains great advice from a range of well-known and successful security practitioners for people looking to enter the cybersecurity field.

Once you have the answers to these questions, compare them to your own circumstances. What might you be able to replicate? What things are nice to know but don't apply to your particular situation? What opportunities do you have that they didn't? The goal here is to find strategies that work for you now, not things that worked for someone else a decade or more ago.

Think of it this way: you are writing your own story. Right now, you are at a starting point. That might be as a high school or college student who is wondering what classes to take. It might be as a mid-career professional who is looking at security as a next career. It might be someone who really doesn't know much about security but wonders if knowing more would help. Regardless of where you start, you need to clear a path to where you want to go. Asking security people how they made their way will give you some ideas and ways of thinking about how to move forward. Writing a story about your own journey will help you know if you are on the right path — even if the story has unplanned twists and turns.

My Story

I never planned to work in security or become a CISO, partly because of when and where I was born. Growing up in the Australian country during the 1970s and 1980s didn't exactly surround me with computer security. I thought I might want to be an English teacher or a landscape architect. But computers? My public high school got their first computers when I was in the 9th grade. Friends played around with Commodore 64s, and I was singularly unimpressed and unaware of the potential of computing.

I wasn't looking to work in technology; technology found me. In my early 20s, after I had moved to the Columbus, Ohio, area, I stumbled into an administrative job. That employer had an old IBM36 mini mainframe and wanted to convert its information to the new client-server software. As the only person in the office under the age of 30, I was thought to be the *perfect* person to work with the small consulting company hired to do the implementation. Later, the owner of that company offered me my first technology job.

I took the opportunity to learn something new. It turns out that I'm good at technology. I spent a great deal of the 1990s building PCs, servers, and networks — a traditional "infrastructure" role. I took a job running help desks and infrastructure for a software development company and got to work helping people learn to use computing technology in their business lives.

I was still not thinking about security. Slowly and subtly, things started to change. The late 1990s introduced me to Y2K issues. The Melissa virus hit while we were struggling to implement Y2K fixes, and then shortly afterward, the Slammer virus became a thing. Even then, I *still* wasn't thinking about security, but I was getting pretty tired of having to chase down bad machines and failing networks. I was getting good at making sure backups worked, having spare parts ready to go, and knowing how to call emergency numbers for support. I didn't know it at the time, but I was starting to do "security."

The pivotal point in my journey happened in the early 2000s. In quick succession, we experienced 9/11 and the North East Power Outage. My CIO asked me to establish a disaster recovery program for the company. Turns out, my personal need for predictability lined up perfectly with being a business continuity and disaster recovery planner. I finally finished college and took these skills to a bank. I was officially working in the world of technology risk. I learned a lot about control frameworks, risk management, and executive leadership. The world was changing, too. Nation-state actors were more cyber active, technology was becoming more ubiquitous at work and at home, and data breaches were starting to become a thing.

After almost 10 years, it was time to find something new. Thanks to my network, I became the CISO at the Ohio State University. There, I learned what it is like to lead a growing security team in a crazy industry. And I learned that I love being a security leader.

But why? It turns out, I like vanilla ice cream. That is, I like things to be dependable, predictable, and reliable.

Running a security program allows me to help an organization ensure that things run according to plan, that they can be depended upon, and that there are no surprises. Being the CISO means that I can have meaningful conversations with senior leaders about why they do what they do and how securing their systems will support their work. Most of all, I can work with security colleagues who value the same things. It's hugely satisfying work.

Create Your Story

There are some high-level truths to keep in mind as you write your security story. These themes will help you be flexible and be able to pivot quickly when a new opportunity arises. If your goal is to find work in the security profession or even continue working in security for years, consider the advice in this chapter.

Align Skills and Strengths

Start by knowing your own "why." (We talk about this later in the book.) Knowing yourself — why you like security, what kind of skills you have, and what culture you want to work in — is the most important thing to have before you start applying for jobs. Nothing will set you up for failure faster than trying to cram your misaligned skills and values into a security role.

When you talk to other people and ask them how they got to where they are, focus on learning their "why." Why do they do security? What do they value about it? What do they not like about it? Reflect on your own values — are they similar? Based on what you know to be important to you, can you see yourself in their role?

Doing security well takes patience, tenacity, and a belief in the purpose of your role. If you can't back that up with your own skills and values, it will be a very hard profession in which to work. Take time to know yourself and have a clear-eyed evaluation of whether this profession is truly for you.

Stay Open to Opportunities

There is no right path for a security career. Even in companies large enough to have defined role-based career ladders, a security practitioner can move up, over, down, and up again in remarkable ways. Often, you will get your next role through who you know and through random opportunities, rather than through a planned career progression.

> Getting your first security job is about playing the numbers game — the more positions you know about and apply for, the more likely it is that you will find a role that works for you.

When you are learning other people's stories, pay attention to how they moved from role to role. Did they intentionally seek a particular job, or did they land in it by accident? Were they comfortable in their choice, or did they have to experience discomfort to move from position to position?

Be curious about new roles, and be open to exploring new opportunities as they come to you. Get to know security people in your immediate team, your company, your location, and your industry. The wider your circle, the more likely you will see when an opportunity arises.

Don't Be Perfect

Be prepared and willing to learn.

The truth is most hiring managers and recruiters write awful job postings for security positions. They require a weird combination of skills and look for educational backgrounds that don't match what the position really requires. Consider the skills they ask for to be aspirational, not required. Until the profession gets better at writing job descriptions, be less concerned about meeting every requirement they ask for and be more concerned about whether you think you can do the job. Later in the book, we will discuss how to form your résumé to get through recruiting filters and catch the eye of hiring managers, so you can get to an interview where you can sell your strengths.

When you meet other people to learn about their path, ask about their skill level when they took a new role. Had they done the role before? Did they consider themselves ready for the new role? Did they have to convince a hiring manager that they were qualified? Learn from their experiences.

Have a general tool kit of skills that can be applied to a variety of potential roles. Hint: Most of the skills are not technical; instead, they are professional skills such as teamwork, accountability, and reliability. Your curiosity about security can be used to learn the fundamentals of security functions. Then you can turn that into a credible job application, even if it does not perfectly match the requirements of the job posting.

Stay Curious

Constant reading, watching, and listening to security thought leaders will help you land a role and help you keep it. There is never a time when you will have "arrived" and you can stop learning. There will be no time where you will feel like you know everything (or even enough of anything). There will always be new technologies, new tactics, and new tools.

Be willing to continue spending time outside of work learning about security things, or it will be easy to fall behind.

The good news is there are lots of ways to learn things: conferences, blogs, podcasts, and books. Be prepared to invest your time in them.

Talk to other people about where they get their information. New sources are emerging all the time. When you do hear/read/learn about something new, take time to process it. If possible, find a way to incorporate it into the job you have now.

If you don't enjoy geeking out on security-related things, this might not be the profession for you. It is not necessary to spend your entire waking life immersed in security — work-life balance is so important — but having a growth/learning mindset is critical.

Network!

Fostering security partners and staying in touch with those colleagues opens more doors than you can count. It's as important a skill as any. Learn how to meet people, establish a connection, and form a mutually beneficial bond. Many times, this will lead to finding true friends. When you're speaking to other security folks, ask them if there is someone they know who you should meet. Ask for an introduction.

Finding your first, second, or next security role will *always* depend on the strength of your network, as will keeping your job. Networking is not something that is an optional part of being in security; it is critical. Your network will act as mentors, teammates, partners, and confidants. There isn't a section of this book that doesn't refer you to a network for guidance and input.

Note that networking does not have to mean in-person schmoozing. You can network on social media, through one-on-one meetings, and by email. In-person networking is the most impactful, but for those who would rather do anything else than mingle, there are other options! If you are looking to get into security, start by finding a local network of people and build outward from there. I make some recommendations for networking groups in the "Resources" appendix at the end of this book.

Pay Your Dues

Working in technology — or any job at all — is invaluable training before you take a role in security. Just because you have a degree or a certification doesn't make you ready for a security job.

> A security professional needs to understand how technology and an organization relate before they can apply security skills and principles to it.

To get a security job, you might need to work elsewhere first. For example, you could've been part of an application development team or a help desk, or you might've worked in compliance or been a business analyst. For many security job seekers, this is the "chicken-and-egg" problem. You need a job to get security skills, and you need skills to get a security job. One way around this is to get a job or internship in areas adjacent to security, such as general IT, business continuity, privacy, audit, or compliance. Once you have those skills, applying for a security role is much easier.

Once you're in a security role, don't be in a hurry to jump around too fast. There is learning to be had in being part of the business cycle for a couple of years. Typically, junior-level people are interested in moving quickly up the career ladder, and in security, there are plenty of opportunities to do just that by jumping from company to company. I suggest taking a more holistic approach so that you fully understand the role. That means staying there for at least a couple of business cycles, which is often a year or two (possibly a bit less if you're at a start-up company). If you are in more of a senior-level position (particularly in a staff management role), this time frame might be even longer. Taking time to truly live in your role will make you a better professional with much deeper skills and experience. Don't overlook the value of this time.

So, You Want to Work in Security

There are a lot of people — young students or mid-career professionals — who are thinking about a career in security. Often, they are overwhelmed by the scope, diversity, and possibility of the profession. Even the people who work in the industry are confused. Is it "information security" or "cybersecurity" or only plain-old "security"? What is included? Is privacy part of security, or is it something separate? What is not included? Is patching part of security, or is it an IT function? It would be reasonable for anyone thinking about joining this profession to have lots of questions.

"Security" is not just one thing any more than "IT," law," or "teaching" are just one thing. It is a broad group of disciplines and specialties that are filled with a diverse set of roles, which span any number of functions. It is based on technology, but it touches on legal, ethics, risk, process, and many more related ideas. It lives in big companies and small ones. It applies to every country and industry — private and public sectors and for-profit and not-for-profit organizations. It bleeds from professional work to our personal lives.

Deciding to work in security brings a plethora of choices, and people considering this field often stumble when working out how and where they want to begin. There are so many questions:

- Should they go to school to learn and then look for a job?
- Should they get a certification first?
- Should they learn on the job and then pursue a formal education or credentials later?
- Should they consider an internship, paid or unpaid, before applying for their first job?
- Should they get a related job like marketing, sales, or help desk and then move into security after that?

There are many potential ways to get into a security role, but few of them are obvious or easy.

It *should* be easy, though. We are constantly told that there are more jobs than people to fill them. Despite the acknowledged huge numbers of openings, there is also a huge shortage of security professionals. You might think it would be easy to get a security job, yes? Unfortunately, it is not so simple. For the security job seeker, the opportunities to break into the profession are circumstantial and capricious. Consider the following:

- There are few truly entry-level, "no experience required" roles in security. When roles like this are available, there are lots of people who apply for them. The competition for any of these entry-level roles is high.
- Most entry-level roles tend to be quite specific, focused on one part of the profession, and are not generalist roles. Hiring managers will want a "network security engineer with knowledge of networks" or an "identity management

analyst with experience in identity systems." They aren't just looking for someone who is "interested in security." Often, security roles are not considered entry level at all. Hiring managers assume you have some other background, usually technical, before you are ready for an entry-level security job. Without those specific skills, it is difficult for a candidate to break into the profession. Without work experience in those areas, many job seekers will not even try to apply for an entry-level role. Job seekers learn that "entry level" often means at least two to three years of work experience — either in security or a related field.

- Many jobs take a long time to fill, if they can be filled at all. Companies and their recruiters might not understand what security is or does, so they post job advertisements that ask for an unrealistic combination of skills and experience (the mythical "unicorn"). If candidates apply at all, they do so knowing that they don't qualify for the stated needs of the role, and for everyone else, there is a missed opportunity to find a role in the industry. This is as true of entry-level roles as it is for mid-level and senior roles.
- Mid-level roles requiring five to ten years of security experience are almost always closed to people already in another part of the workforce who want to transfer over to security. Those kinds of transfers most often happen at companies where the hiring manager knows the transferring candidate. Being able to transfer mid-career without years of security experience is rare (but not impossible!).
- Mid-level and senior security jobs are hot, and candidates expect higher salaries and benefits than other information technology jobs. Companies, however, do not value security roles the same way and don't pay what job seekers are expecting. As a result, the time to fill a position (and the

time to find a job that pays appropriately) is long, and there are many instances of job-hopping for higher pay.

- Senior security leadership roles are high-burnout positions. The average tenure of a CISO is roughly two years. Not only does this make finding good senior talent hard to find, but it also makes the stability of the rest of the security organization less dependable. This impacts the frequency and quality of all open positions being advertised.

Despite many security jobs being posted, it is a challenge for the job seeker to find the right kind of job in the right place at the right time. To deal with this, you need to be ready for any potential opportunity that arises. It can be done! Once you have a security job, it is easier to move around to other roles. Getting a foot in the security door is the hardest step.

The task of being prepared can seem overwhelming, but there are many resources available to help you, and there are many examples of people successfully finding their way into security.

What's Next?

- Spend some time thinking about why you are interested in security. Be honest with yourself. Do you like playing with technology? Does the role of defender appeal to you? Maybe someone you admire is a security professional, and you would like to emulate them. Perhaps the potential earnings and job security are attractive. Jot down your answers, and then take some time to reflect on them. Do they feel right?
- Find people on social media who are doing jobs you are interested in. Check out their backgrounds and experience. Connect with and engage them in a meet-and-greet. Ask your network for introductions.

- Look at job postings for the kinds of jobs you want. Take note of the skills and experience they are seeking. Do you have those skills and experience? Do you *want* to have those skills and experience? Consider ways of filling in the gaps in your experience and skills.
- Look for networking groups and security meetups in your area. Attend a meeting. Introduce yourself to at least one person while you are there. Make a list of questions to ask anyone you meet. Be prepared to engage someone in meaningful conversation at a networking event or function.
- Read *Confident Cyber Security: How to Get Started in Cyber Security and Future Proof Your Career* by Dr. Jessica Barker, for more ideas for breaking into security.

CHAPTER 2

Why Security?

Summary

- **Know yourself:** It's important to know why you value security, know your strengths and values, and then find connections between them.
- **Learn about security:** There are cultures within security — protectors, puzzlers, moral crusaders, and change agents. Do any of these resonate with you?
- **Do some research:** Understand your strengths. Talk to friends, family, and colleagues, and ask for their thoughts on what you are good at and what you struggle with. Compare this to the security roles you are interested in, and make sure there is an overlap between the skills needed and your strengths.

- **Be clear:** Be clear about why security matters and why it matters to other people. Put yourself in others' shoes to understand how they perceive security.

"I can't believe anyone would want to do security." —Interviewer

In the late 2000s, I interviewed for a security role in an imposing office overlooking Park Avenue in New York. The interview was with a senior technology officer with a sharp suit and a great reputation. I was nervous! Imagine my surprise when the first statement from the interviewer cast doubt on the whole premise for my job and career.

I would love to tell you that this opinion was an anomaly. It wasn't. The attitude reflected their ignorance of security and the lack of value they placed on the security function. They were not alone in sharing this opinion — not then and not now. One of the biggest causes of conflict and stress when working in security is when others misunderstand what security is or why security people make the decisions they make. They think we are recalcitrant, obstinate, or downright annoying. We think we are helping them avoid something they cannot see, preparing them to achieve their objectives without an unanticipated security incident, and helping them to be better. In all cases, these instances of disagreement arise because we don't understand the others' "why."

We security people think the purpose of security is obvious and that any semi-intelligent life form would understand why security is important. The truth is that security is a profession that is misunderstood by technologists and nontechnologists alike.

> If you're going to be part of or lead a security team, you need to be very clear about why you do it, what value it brings, and how security is a good thing.

If you don't believe this with the core of your being, you will likely burn out well before you can be successful.

For someone starting out in this profession, finding a "why" can be difficult. It's hard to find a "why" when you don't know the "what" or the "how." One place to start is by reading Simon Sinek's book *Start with Why*. It is not a security book, but it will help you think about what drives you, what is important, and how security might fit into your life. For now, your "why" answer might simply be "because I'm curious to learn more" or "I like what I see so far."

What Kind of People Do Security?

Work in security long enough, and you will notice particular security cultures and subcultures. Being able to align your values with the culture you work in is important. It is too hard to go to work every day if you must flex your personality to fit in. So, consider the kind of security personas who already work in security and see if your values and style align with any of them.

There are four types of security personas.

Security Personas

	Protector	Puzzler	Moral Crusader	Change Agent
Cares About	Community service	Intellectual pursuit	Ethics and fairness	New challenges
Leadership Style	National defense	Strategic planner	Values-driven	Fixer
Junior Roles	Blue team/ incident response	Red team/security analyst	Governance, risk, and policy	All roles but not for long

The Protector

These people might come from a military or other service background. They see security as a community service that enables our freedoms and organizational mission. They often refer to security as a "battlefield," and they are combatants who defend an organization. Security workers with this mindset gravitate toward issues of nation-state attacks and are personally engaged in security operations and other incident response activities. Newer security professionals enjoy security training and awareness, security intelligence, and security operations. Not surprisingly, you often find them in national cyber defense organizations, but you can find them in most industries and locations.

People starting out in security often start in defense-related ("blue team") roles. These are great places to learn how security works, learn what it really takes to "defend" an organization from cyberattacks, and generally get a feel for the bulk of security functions. Having a protector tendency is good for these kinds of roles.

The Puzzler

Being part of a security program, function, or service is an intellectual and complicated pursuit. Some people are attracted to security for this challenge alone. These professionals prioritize strategic planning and enjoy the interaction of policy, politics, and organizational management. They are in it for the long game, recognizing that there might be minor setbacks along the way. They might enjoy reverse engineering, penetration testing, or engineering design. In all cases, they love that they are surrounded by smart people who are doing unique things.

You might fall into this category if you are constantly learning new technologies, fascinated by technological advances, or interested in data analysis to solve complicated problems. Puzzlers tend to become subject-matter experts in a particular field — because they go deep in their learning. If you are a puzzler, look for roles with teammates you can learn from and a company that will support your thirst for knowledge.

The Moral Crusader

Like ethics? So does this security professional. They see their role as one that ensures the way we manage systems and information is ethical and appropriate. They are closely aligned to their privacy peers and often talk about values-driven security. They believe security to be one of the bedrock elements of a good organization. Security crusaders are attracted to governance and risk roles, including frameworks and policy.

People in this category are rule makers and rule followers. They demand rules to ensure fairness and predictability. They want to know that people are being secure according to guidelines and best practices. They believe security is not the end goal; instead, they see security as a way to ensure fairness and trustworthiness in a system or company.

The Change Agent

Many in the security profession, newbies and leaders alike, will tell you that one of the appeals of security is that it is always changing. This is also one of the things that frustrates nonsecurity leaders the most. ("When will we be done with security stuff?") Security people who like change will use the ever-changing nature of technology and its related security elements as security team value propositions. That is, when the business changes, so do the threats and vulnerabilities. Therefore, the company really needs security.

Security people will often use the changing nature of technology and security to learn new skills and take new roles. You will find change agents in all kinds of security roles.

People who are change agents often consider themselves to be "fixers." They take on project after project, moving from one job to the next relatively quickly. They get bored with doing the same thing for too long.

What Is Your Why?

Like all personality types, few people fall into just one category. Most of us have a piece of each type and use them at different times in our careers.

If you are just getting into security, you should have a sense of your "why" and have a sense of the type of job that will align with your style. It will help guide you to the parts of security that will align with your primary values. Over time, your "why" might change, and that is okay. Just know that you will be better at security, have more fun, and get less stressed if you know why you're there in the first place.

When you are talking to a hiring manager, try to find out their "why." It will help you find someone who will be aligned with your values and make your day-to-day working life better. Even if they emphasize a category that you don't, simply knowing what they value will help you better manage your working relationship.

So, how about you? What is your "why"? If you're not sure, consider doing the things discussed in the following sections.

Think About It

Take some time to do some real introspection to try to articulate your core values. What is most important to you? Why are those things so important? I'm not just talking about security values; I'm talking about the whole enchilada — family, faith, money, status, location, education/learning, and so on.

What are your strengths? Are you a communicator, an analyst, or an artist? Strengths are not things you've mastered; instead, think of them as things you like to do, things that you are comfortable doing (most of the time), and things that energize you. Consider reading *Now, Discover Your Strengths* by Marcus Buckingham and Donald Clifton.

If you have trouble getting started, consider thinking about the negatives, such as what values and strengths you don't have. This can help narrow down the strengths and values you have, and it will let you choose security roles that avoid the things that bring you no joy.

Introspection takes effort and is something that you should revisit regularly, because while your values might be stable, your strengths can change over time.

Make a List

Keep it handy. Talk to family, friends, and co-workers. Ask them to be honest when giving you feedback. What do they think you value? What do they think your strengths are?

Do the things they call out as your strengths match your own list? If they do, great! It is not unusual for them to raise something you haven't thought of, so feel free to add it to your list. Sometimes, you might be surprised or disagree. This is a great opportunity to really take time to investigate your own feelings on the matter. Others might be wrong, and you're certainly allowed to disregard their input. But if enough people call something out that surprises you, you might have a strength or value that you should include in your deliberations.

You might also have something on your list that they don't mention, so ask them about these, too. You might have something you think is a strength that really isn't. You might also have a strength that you're not making visible. This is valuable information to have! Examine any of these disconnects. This might be something you think is valuable that really isn't. Maybe something you take for granted is admired by others. Feedback is a gift, so take it in all its forms.

Link It to Security

What is it about security that you like? What do you not like?

If you are not already in security, a bit of research is in order. Use Cyberseek.org to look at the different kinds of roles in security. Read some magazines or blogs and listen to some podcasts. (Check out the "Resources" appendix at the end of the book for some suggestions.) See what kind of roles and topics are (or aren't) attractive to you and write them down. If you can, do some interviews with folks already in security to help you learn more about what they do. Attend a conference or two. You'll start getting a general sense of what is out there.

If you're already in security, you likely already have an opinion. As you take note of your likes and dislikes, also consider why you like/dislike something. Do you like the people you work with? Do you like the conditions of the job (steady-state, constantly changing, or other)?

Once you have a list of potential security roles, step back and look at it objectively. You might see themes emerging (perhaps you like working solo, doing research, and the like) that weren't obvious before. Great!

Know Why Security Is Valuable

Why do you think security is a valuable function in your organization or community?

This one is harder to answer. You need to put yourself in other people's shoes. Why would/should your family care about security? Why would your nonsecurity teammates care? Why would organizational leaders care? What about your customers?

You need to think through this because if you are going to have a job in security, you must know if the people around you understand why and what you do. If everyone agrees security is important, your career path will be much easier. I haven't found any place like this yet!

If you decide that others don't think security is important, it is still okay to pursue a security job. However, how you describe what you do and what kind of support community you set up will be different. You will need to be prepared to meet some resistance along the way and to deal with it.

You and Security

Here is the hard part: compare your list of values with the security values list. How do your core values and your security value statements line up? Do they? If they don't, why not?

Ideally, you will see significant overlap between the two. An overlap is a potential career path for you to pursue. If you identify that you value security for how it protects the organization from threats, that you like doing threat analysis, and that the company values being protected from threats, then all things are in alignment. Great! On the other hand, if you really like communicating security things to people and the company culture would rather not know about potentially threatening things, then it is not so great. Doing security training and awareness can be good, but it might not be so good at your current company. If you are interviewing for a position at a new company, you should ask about this during the interview to ensure your values align with the company's values.

When you have your answers, use them to guide your career and to strengthen you when the going gets tough. We all need a guiding light. What is yours?

What's Next?

If you are thinking about working in security or have been working in security for a decade or more, now is the time to answer the questions raised in this chapter. Identify your strengths, the value you place on security, and the kind of jobs that amplify your strengths. Time spent on this will pay off in making sure you find a role in which you can succeed and be happy.

CHAPTER

3

Where Can I Begin?

Summary

- **Research:** There is no agreed-upon career path for security and no commonly understood way of doing security. This can make it confusing for a person who is starting out.
- **More research:** Security jobs can be core security teams or in functions adjacent to security (such as legal, business analysis, or communications teams). Understand what roles are adjacent to security that might become pathways for you.
- **Even more research:** Check out Cyberseek.org and other websites to understand security jobs and the skills

needed to do them. Review mindmaps to understand how they all fit together.

- **Know yourself:** Understand your comfort level with technology and how much business experience you have. Talk to security people who do what interests you and learn how they got there.

When people start thinking about working in security, they often begin by thinking that they want to work in security based on the ideas of a single person, such as the hacker or a single role they've seen (such as a pentester or analyst). Maybe they know and admire someone who works in security and think they'd like to be like that person. Perhaps they have heard that there are a lot of jobs available in security and think it could be a solid career to pursue.

So, they start looking at job postings, descriptions of roles, or security frameworks. They quickly learn that *security* is a term that encompasses many different types of roles, and soon they are overwhelmed with options. They look at the skills and experience required and realize they don't have most of the skills needed, even for entry-level jobs. The catch-22 is that you need a job to get the skills, but you need the skills to get the job.

And then they might get stuck. Why is this so difficult?

If you want to study medicine, law, or accounting, your path is well-defined. You go to college and get a (graduate) degree in your field, and then you sit for a professional exam that will certify you to work in the industry. And then you go to work in that industry and take continuing education to maintain your license. You don't have much choice. For these professions, their canon was created a long time ago, and schools have been created with licensing and professional requirements in mind. Security is different — for some good reasons.

Unlike professions like medicine, accounting, or law, security doesn't have a professional requirement of degrees, skills, or licensing. The security profession is still young, and companies and institutions are still making it up as they go along. There is no one place to go to look for a definitive guide to security careers. There are no generally accepted security principles to learn about and follow, and there are no commonly understood security codes of conduct.

There is no commonly understood organizational structure for security. Talk to any security leader about the functions on their team, and you will get a wide variety of answers. Do they manage identity management, or is that handled by the IT team? Are they responsible for disaster recovery, or is someone else responsible for that? Who is responsible for security compliance? What about third-party risk management? Is security risk its own risk area within the enterprise risk structure, or is it part of operational risk? Sometimes, what you might think of as a security function really belongs elsewhere in the organization — but maybe not.

How security is viewed by the rest of the business varies significantly. Sometimes, the security team (including the leader) is buried in the technology organization, and all job roles are written in terms of IT. Sometimes, security is part of the compliance organization, or security personnel report to the chief financial officer or are part of the business risk group. Sometimes, if you're really lucky, the security leader reports directly to the CEO, and their career stack is independent of anything else. Where the security function sits in the organization determines how the security career path might look.

It can be truly frustrating for someone who is new to the industry and who is trying to figure out what kind of roles there are, how much growth potential they have, and where to begin.

What Does It Mean to Be a Security Professional?

Most of the time, when people are thinking about "working in security," they think first about working in support of an organization's security. Of course, there are other kinds of roles, but typically, that's not what comes to mind first. They imagine being part of the team that helps make an organization more secure and that reports to a chief information security officer (CISO) or another leader. In this world, there are ways to think about jobs that focus on these internal groups, as you'll learn in the coming sections.

Technical Security: Blue Teams and Red Teams

Blue teams are operational defenders of an organization. Blue team roles include incident responders and security engineers for endpoints, identity, application development, networks, cloud, forensics, threat intelligence, and so on. Blue team technical roles can also include auditing and compliance, or they can include governance and policy. The role of blue teams is to create ways to protect the people, technology, and information being used by an organization. When looking for blue team jobs, look for terms like *security operations*, *security architecture*, *risk assessment*, or *threat intelligence* as a place to start.

Red teams discover system and process weaknesses. They might do testing to exploit those weaknesses and to help the organization improve its security controls. Penetration testers, vulnerability researchers, threat hunters, and others make up red teams that partner with blue teams. When searching for red team jobs, look for *pentesting*, *ethical hacking*, *reverse engineering*, and *threat intelligence*. (I know, threat intelligence is on the blue team side, too.)

Nontechnical Security

No one is ever far from technology in security, but there are roles where the skill of the role is less focused on technical security and is focused more on human/legal/business processes. Such roles exist to ensure the organization is managed with security in mind. These roles include security analysts, security compliance officers, operational risk managers, training and awareness analysts, or security business analysts. Typically, these roles are found in governance, risk, and compliance (GRC) functions and entry-level jobs that are also posted as "analyst" roles.

Frequently, people in these roles will work with security frameworks — to understand regulatory requirements and apply them to internal company policies and procedures. They align, directly or indirectly, with legal areas like compliance. There is often an overlap with blue teams, so in some companies, the teams are organizationally separate, while in other companies, they are combined into one.

Look for terms like *governance, risk, and compliance (GRC)*, *security policy*, and *information risk* for the more nontechnical roles in security.

Adjacent Spaces

Like every function in an organization, security must work with people who do adjacent work. Security people rely heavily on communications and marketing groups. Security people also need support from the training and awareness staff. Project and program managers are indispensable. Financial and human resource support is critical for directly working with and within security. Again, in some organizations, these people are all under one security organizational umbrella; in others, they are separate functions. Regardless, an entire security team needs all these functions to operate properly.

There are also other partners whose work will influence security. Enterprise risk management, privacy, business continuity management, IT operations, sales, and marketing are functions that are separate from security, though they are very important to the success of the security program. The decisions these leaders make will set the strategy and work plans for the security team. In larger companies, people from these groups often liaise directly with security teams.

Security Product Companies

In addition to security teams that work within an organization, there are companies that produce security tools and services. Some CISOs consider these to be an extension of their own red/blue teams. Within these security product companies, everyone working in the organization is "working in security." Roles such as product design or sales are integral to that security ecosystem. Of course, these companies are looking for people with deep technical security backgrounds to produce and support their products and their own companies, but they will also need many people without security backgrounds. These companies can be a great place to get your foot in the door to learn more about the security field without necessarily starting with direct security defense or offense experience.

How Can You Make Sense of It All?

Before you send out your résumé to a hiring manager, consider the information in the following sections.

Website Resources

Check out Cyberseek.org and the Workforce Framework for Cybersecurity (NICE Framework) Work Roles table (https://niccs.us-cert.gov/nice-cybersecurity-workforce-framework-work-roles) to learn about security job classifications and skill requirements. These are new resources that try to codify the security profession. Fair warning: they are still very much a work in progress, but they are a great place to start.

Cyberseek.org, for example, provides resources to job seekers, employers, educators, and students. Its purpose is to help learn what kind of jobs and careers exist and what kind of skills are required for those jobs. The site bases its pathways on jobs currently posted, so it might not give you a long-term future vision. Regardless, this is a great place to do your homework.

In the United States, the federal government has created the National Initiative for Cybersecurity Education (NICE) framework (https://www.nist.gov/itl/applied-cybersecurity/nice). The framework itself is a chunky document to read. (I would recommend it only if you really wanted to geek out on it.) However, there are lots of good summary resources on the NICE website, which will help you learn about the types of job roles and the skills required to do those jobs. It is very federal government-focused, which means it doesn't explore private-sector security company jobs like product managers, marketing, or sales, but it is adding more all the time.

Cybersecurity Mindmaps

A mindmap is simply a visualization of a concept. Cybersecurity mindmaps are a visualization of the functions that make up cybersecurity, usually presented in the format of a CISO organization or the roles a CISO must cover. Do an internet search for *Cybersecurity Mindmap* and look at the images. I like the ones produced by Rafeeq Rehman at http://rafeeqrehman.com/.

There is no one mindmap that is definitively correct, so don't just look at one. Instead, look at a few to see common areas. For example, most security mindmaps include functions like "risk assessment," "governance, risk, and compliance," or "security operations." In many mindmaps, you will find functions like "training and awareness," "pentesting," or "auditing." Sometimes, the pentesting can be listed under "operations," and sometimes, you will see it under "risk management."

As you check these out, consider your own skills and interests, and note any area that looks appealing to you. If you see a new term or one you don't know much about, do more research.

Your Technical Experience

Consider the amount of technical experience you already have.

There are many security job seekers who have "technical" backgrounds. By that, I mean they know something about computers. Maybe they know a programming language, how to build networks, or how to run their own websites. That's great. There are plenty of security jobs that will use those skills. If you have technology skills, this is the place to begin.

Many people don't have that kind of background at all. Maybe they have project management skills. Maybe they are great at music, are a trained teacher, or have a law degree. There are roles in security for them, too.

You do *not* have to be technical to have a role in security.

Functions like governance, risk, compliance, user awareness, or access management all lend themselves to people without deep technical knowledge. People who enjoy improving processes, connecting people and problems, and understanding legal and regulatory matters know how psychology works in making risk decisions. They also know that all the things that make humans tick are needed in security.

> You *will* have to be comfortable with and learn something about technology to work in security.

If you are not comfortable with technology and working with technologists, it will be more difficult for you to find a path into security and to be successful. Being comfortable with technology means being relaxed using computers and being willing to learn about new technology as it emerges. It means being willing to try new technology and talk with technologists about how things work. At a high level, it means understanding the history and future of technology, how and why security fits into technology, and general computing and security principles.

Your General Business Experience

Consider the amount of general business experience you already have. Perhaps you have other skills that would help you move into security. Some security-adjacent skills include business analysis, training, education, psychology, project management, or data analytics.

Simply having work experience in any industry, location, or field can be your starting point. Have you sold burgers in the fast-food industry? Reach out to security teams in the restaurant industry and sell your customer-facing experience. Have you run some projects for a state government? Talk to the security teams in that organization or any other public organization and sell your project management *and* public-sector experience. Leverage what you know about those industries to learn about the kind of security issues they face. Look for places where your business skills and their security issues overlap. Start there.

Interview Security People

A great place to start learning about security is by talking to people who work in the industry to get their stories. Go to a conference like a local BSides (http://www.securitybsides.com/w/page/12194156/FrontPage) or ISSA (www.issa.org) event. You could also attend a local security meet-up, or you can ask your LinkedIn or social media contacts. What do they do? How did they learn how to do it? Where do they think opportunities exist for you to enter the field? You don't have to buy everyone coffee, but you do have to make an effort to reach out virtually or in person.

Many security people love talking about their experiences and are excited to help new people join the industry. Take advantage of the community.

Note that while it is great to talk to security leaders about their journey, just know that their experiences won't be anything like yours. Make sure you also find people who are new to security or are two to five years into their careers. They will be able to give you the most current and relevant experience. This is where having a membership in local professional organizations can really help.

What's Next?

If you haven't already done it, now is the time to do some research. Look at job postings and do some internet searching on *cybersecurity jobs* and *information security jobs*. Get a feel for the kind of jobs available in your chosen locations. Think about whether you are interested in blue team, red team, or adjacent jobs. Talk to people in security, online, or in person. Ask questions.

CHAPTER

4

What Training Should I Take?

Summary

- **Know yourself:** There is no standard training for security. Design your own path based on what you want to do, where you are starting from, and how much time you have to devote to training.
- **Research:** Understand what kinds of training is available, how much it costs, and what type of training suits the kinds of security roles you are pursuing. Traditional students are safe pursuing a degree. Mid-career people might consider a degree, but it might be faster and

more efficient to consider boot camps or other shorter-term training.

- **Network:** Talk to security people about different training options and learn what they value and why.

There is no right path to getting into security. For some, getting into security is a series of happy accidents, a case of right place, right time, with a bit of hard work thrown into the mix. For others, they work intentionally to get the right skills, meet the right people, and muscle their way into a security job. For most security job seekers, working with intention is likely the more successful path. The "happy accident" doesn't seem to happen as often anymore. It's true that everyone will need to pay their dues, hard work will get you a long way, and good luck might take you further. But these days, it is less likely a manager will call you and ask you to learn on the job (not impossible but less likely). Having a plan to break into security might be a better option.

Many security job seekers start by evaluating their current knowledge and exploring training options. Security has a lot of options to choose from!

- You could go to college to get a degree in security (no programs are the same), but that's not necessary.
- You could go to a boot camp to learn security skills.
- You could start work doing something else (often somewhere in IT but not necessarily) and maybe do some on-the-job training before moving laterally into a security role.
- You could be a senior leader (usually in IT or risk areas) and adopt security into your work portfolio.
- You just know someone.

There is no single path to follow, so my advice to a job seeker is to consider where you are starting from.

For the Traditional Student

In some ways (and especially these days), this is an easier path. If you want to get into security (or know someone who is interested), there are traditional programs that can be followed.

- Most (but not all) security disciplines start in technology, so in elementary/high school, pursue programs that will lead you to computer science, such as robotics, math, and computers (of course). However, don't forget writing and analysis skills! You could go straight from there to a junior IT position and move over to security once you have some experience under your belt.
- Many colleges and universities offer information/cybersecurity programs (both two- and four-year options). Two-year options will be more practical, often with industry certificates attached. Four-year colleges will be deeper and broader, often with internship opportunities included. I would *highly* recommend that you find ways to take non-computer science electives whenever you can. Skills in writing, psychology, data analytics, ethics, and policy play a *huge* role in experienced security positions, so take advantage of these classes when you can find them.
- Even with a degree, recruiting managers prefer someone with work experience, and experience in a security job is even better. So, find ways to do internships while you're at school if you can. (Often, the college security team will hire students, so start there.) It's a bonus if you attend a school that gives you course credit for doing an internship!

- If you get to the end of a four-year program without having any work experience, I recommend heading into the workforce from there before considering any post-graduate degree programs. The reality is that most security jobs don't require a four-year degree at all (at least, they shouldn't!) and certainly won't require a master's-level degree for junior roles. You also need to make sure you can apply the theory of the classroom to the reality of the workplace. You will see that the accepted theory of "patch all the things" never happens in the real world!
- If you already have an undergraduate degree, you might be asking whether getting a master's or other post-grad security degree might be beneficial. My answer? It depends on what your undergraduate degree is in. If your undergraduate is already in a computing-related field such as computer science, management information systems, or computer engineering, you are likely qualified enough to land an entry-level security role. Take the time to get work experience before pursuing a higher-level degree. On the other hand, if your degree is not related to computing, it might be worth considering a post-graduate program, certificate, or master's program in security.

For the Nontraditional Student

A nontraditional student is one who is headed back to school as a more mature adult. Often, they juggle part-time work and family while trying to learn. This isn't an easy path, so I recommend finding ways of learning that support your lifestyle as efficiently as possible.

- Here's where industry certifications can be good thing about industry certs is that they can g learning roadmap. They will show you the knowledge you need to be considered educated in a security topic. Regardless of how you get the certification, just the act of learning the material is résumé-worthy. Studying for industry certifications can be self-paced, online, or via a book, or they can be done with a weeklong boot camp, though they include an investment of money and time.
- Regardless of whether they result in a certification, boot camps can be a good jump start into getting skills you need — if you have the time to attend them. Some of these camps span many full-time weeks and are not suited to someone who is already working, but they are worth checking out if you have the time to spend. Some industry groups, such as ISSA.org, have local chapters that offer part-time evening training on certifications at a very reasonable price. These are also great networking opportunities!
- Part-time/online college can be useful if you don't already have an undergrad degree. If you already have a two- or four-year degree in something else, I wouldn't suggest doing another undergrad degree in security or computer science. Professional certificates or post-grad certificates would be a quicker and cheaper option.

For the Full-Time Nonsecurity Worker

If you are already working but not in security and want to move over to a security role, I encourage you to start at your current company (if it is big enough). Without leaving your current position, find ways to get to know the security team — and work with them if you can. Ask them for guidance on the skills they need and the positions they will be looking to fill. You might already have program management, IT support, or risk management skills. Adding a small amount of security knowledge might set you up to move over to the team when the next opportunity arises.

If you don't work in a company with a security team (or the security team isn't one you want to join), use your networking capabilities (see more on this below) to find other options.

Consider taking a self-paced training class. There are many options available, such as YouTube, LinkedIn Learning, and others, as well as a variety of books. This can be a great way to learn on a timetable that works for you, though I would encourage you to work with a mentor to determine what kind of training is worthwhile for the type of job you are pursuing.

Other Things to Consider

Regardless of what kind of student you are or how much time you have to spend, there are ways of learning about security that take place outside a classroom. The following items can help you round out your learning on your way to your security career.

Certifications

Here's the truth about security certifications: You rarely need them to do a security job, but you might need them to get a security job *in the first place*. A certification gets you through recruiting filters and might distinguish you from similar candidates.

> Having a certification or degree signals to a potential employer that you're interested enough in the profession that you've invested time and resources to learn more about it. It doesn't mean that you have the skills to do the job itself.

Some certifications are quite general (CISSP, CISA, CompTIA+, and so on), and some are quite specific (cloud certifications, ethical hacking, and the like). Choose your certification based on what role you want to land, and look at job postings for that job to see what certifications/skills they're requiring.

Many certifications require you to pass a test and have years of experience working in the subject matter area. Don't worry! If you are just starting out, learning the material and passing the test is excellent for your résumé and general learning curve. It's okay to note on your résumé that you are pursuing a certification, even if you don't yet have the work experience to earn the piece of paper. As you see in the following table, there are certifications for everyone from the entry-level job seeker to the seasoned professional:

Certifications

Type	Cost	Good For
Entry Level		
CompTIA: Security+, A+, Linux+	$	Basic security concepts. Used by the U.S. federal government for contract work. Incident response analysts and general risk analysts use these.

(Continued)

Type	Cost	Good For
Cisco CCNA: Network Administration	$	Basic network security.
Industry Certifications		
ISACA: Security Auditing (CISA); Security Management (CISM)	$$	Auditing and general security management.
ISC2: Security Professional (CISSP)	$$	Industry standard for any blue/red team role.
Technical Certifications		
SANS: Security Essentials (GSEC); Pentesting & Ethical Hacking (GPEN); Application Pentesting (GWAPT)	$$$	Technically respected. Great for SOC analysts, pentesters, ethical hackers.
Offensive Security (OSCP)	$$$	Pentesting.
CREST: Malware Reverse Engineering (CMRE)	$$	Malware analyst.
Cloud Security Alliance (CCSK)	$	Cloud security.

Networking

No matter where you start, you cannot underestimate the value of networking! If you are a traditional student, start with the student organizations that do security things, such as security clubs, women in security, and capture-the-flag competitions. If there isn't one at your school, start one, and put that on your résumé. For anyone seeking a security job, attend local security conferences or professional groups in your area. Getting to know the organizations and hiring managers will give you early warning of job openings and will often get you past recruiting roadblocks. Don't be shy to let people know that you're looking for a security job, and be clear about what type of security job you're looking for. It takes time and energy, but it is completely worth it.

Job Shadowing

Some people take time to do job shadowing. Job shadowing can be a good way to learn more about what a "day in the life" of a security person is and learn more about a particular type of security job. If you are time-constrained, I would caution you against spending time doing this. It is hard to learn much by following someone around, because it takes time to understand the organizational context. Because of confidentiality, the person you are shadowing often can't share meaningful information. Also, people who are shadowed are often more junior people who don't yet know how to communicate their roles. Also, you might end up job shadowing a senior leader who does things you probably won't do (for a while).

Having said all that, the biggest benefit to job shadowing is, you guessed it, networking. It's an opportunity for them to get to know you and have you top of mind when a job opens up. I can think of more efficient ways to network, but consider job shadowing if you have the time to spend.

Types of Training

The security training market is growing and changing. Some companies have partnered with colleges and boot camps to create a security curriculum specifically for their company and pay their employees to attend. Some larger companies are creating their own security certificates that they will honor in place of a four-year degree. Professional organizations like ISSA partner to offer reduced-cost training and boot camps to their members. You now can take many varieties of training, so find the kind that works best for your current circumstance. The following table shows you the pros and cons of your options:

Types of Training

Type	Pros	Cons
Boot camps	Short time frame; current technology; links to hiring managers	Can be expensive for the time spent; might not be recognized by hiring managers.
Two-year degree	Practical skill focus; often linked to industry certs; cheaper tuition	Might not be sufficient for some hiring managers.
Four-year degree	Deeper technical learning; long time to complete, particularly for part-time students	Difficult to stay current with emerging technologies; might be too focused on theory at the expense of practical experience.
Self-paced training	Fastest option; cheap/free; fits with a busy lifestyle	Might not be recognized by hiring managers; might not be targeted to the desired job.
Internships	Practical experience is highly valued by hiring managers; good for networking	Benefits are highly dependent on the quality of the program.

Despite all the press about the thousands of open security jobs waiting to be filled, getting any security job is a serendipitous combination of skill, location, company need, and timing, which means that finding the right job takes time. Be prepared to apply to as many jobs as possible to maximize your opportunities. Also, be prepared to apply to jobs that you might not be completely qualified for. (More on this in Chapter 6, "Is My Résumé Okay?") The more senior the role, the longer you should expect the job search and interviewing/hiring process to take.

What's Next?

- Evaluate your formal learning about security. If you have none, consider your options.
- If you're in college but not doing a security major/minor, talk to your adviser about classes you could take that touch on security/risk concepts.
- Find local networking groups in your area and connect with them. Once connected, find someone in the group to meet with and ask about what they do.
- If you work in a company with a security team, ask the leader to meet with you. Find out if you can job shadow for a day.
- Investigate and sign up for security training/certification options that will work for your budget and lifestyle.

CHAPTER

5

What Skills Should I Have?

Summary

- **Know yourself:** Based on your strengths and desired roles, choose a piece of the technology stack to begin your technical skills training. Plan on focusing there for at least a year or two.
- **Know yourself more:** How is your emotional intelligence? Get feedback from co-workers, friends, and family. Where do you need to grow?
- **Network:** Ask your network what kinds of skills they think you need for the kinds of jobs you want to get. Practice presenting security topics in front of them.

The pursuit of security knowledge and applying that knowledge for security skills is part of every security role at every level of an organization. When seeking a security job for the first time, it is important to know which skills to have and the order in which to learn them.

There are many security leaders who value candidates who start with a generic technical or business background before moving into security. Many hiring managers feel that security is inherently *not* an entry-level role. Instead, these hiring managers think being an analyst or engineer requires general technology skills and business experience that are found outside the security function. As more schools offer security degrees and certificates, this might change. Regardless, finding a candidate who has spent time building networks, coding, or working on a help desk is vastly superior to hiring someone straight out of school without that background.

> Regardless of where you start, you will never stop honing your security skills or learning new general skills.

As you progress through your career, the kind of training will change. You might start by learning basic security concepts and applying them to basic security tasks. You might continue to learn a lot about one piece of security, becoming a subject-matter expert (SME) in that one function. You can branch out to related security functions and associated skills, leveraging what you already learned to take a slightly different path. Later, you might manage a team, which will require you to spend more time honing generic management skills, such as team leadership, organizational design, budgeting, and so on, even as you keep learning new security tools and tactics. As a leader, you might need to improve your communication, influence, and strategy skills.

Many people are initially attracted to the profession because of someone they know or something they've seen. They might be attracted by the thought of being a security analyst, finding vulnerabilities in technology as part of bug bounty projects. (Bug bounty platforms provide a way for companies to engage with analysts who discover [and are compensated for] vulnerabilities in company software.) They might be enticed by a TV show in which someone seamlessly traverses public databases looking for criminals. Perhaps they have worked with someone in security, admired their work, and thought this could be a good career to move into. Or perhaps they've just noticed the salaries of security engineers in various surveys and thought that this could be a stepping-stone to a higher standard of living.

Regardless of the initial attraction, once folks start investigating the security profession, they are almost always surprised at how many kinds of roles there are. They might have thought of security as one technology pillar among other pieces of technology (applications, servers, or networks) and are amazed to find out that there are many more pieces to security (analyst, engineer, governance, sales, law, awareness, policy, and so on).

All these choices can be a bit overwhelming. Where to start? How to proceed?

The Entry Point — Technology

Most security positions assume you have worked in a technology field. At one time, there was a preference for infrastructure skills, particularly networking skills. Now, the preference seems to be software and integrations. Regardless of whether you start at the bottom of the technology stack or at the top, security remains a technology function at its core. Figure 5.1 shows how the layers of the OSI technology stack interrelate. Consider whether you know much about any of these layers, and consider security roles that focus on those pieces of technology.

What Kind of Technology Skills?

There is no wrong answer to this question. Go back to your values and strengths. Historically, the most common security technology skills start with a focus on the technology stack (networking, systems administration, or coding). Learning how the technological plumbing works is important if you're going to defend or attack it.

As the profession has expanded, so has the hardware and technologies we care about. Items like the cloud (infrastructure, platform, and application) are newer but here to stay. The Internet of Things (IoT) is exploding, so how do we secure all the things connected to the internet? Operational technology (OT) security is a subset of security that is focused on securing critical infrastructure systems (water, power, and so on) and is key to protecting national security. What will it be like to work in OT security as nation-state cyberattacks continue to grow?

Layer	Function
Application	• Network Process to Application
Presentation	• Data Representation and Encryption
Session	• Interhost Communications
Transport	• End-to-End Connections and Reliability
Network	• Path Determination and IP (Logical Addressing)
Data	• MAC and LLC (Physical Addressing)
Physical	• Media, Signal, and Binary Transition

FIGURE 5.1 OSI technology stack model

Many students coming from college are f
cation security. While application security inv
also about systems integrations, reverse engineer
hacking. I would suggest that some level of coding is going to be crucial for most security careers. If you want to have a long career in security, it will be important for you to be able to build websites or tools and be able to deal with the huge amounts of data you will undoubtedly encounter. And having those skills is a big advantage for job seekers. There is debate about the right kind of programming language to choose (Python? C++? HTML? Other?). Again, check out the kind of jobs you're looking for to see what kind of languages are needed or talk to security teams to get their opinion.

If you are choosing to go deep into a technical security career, consider getting access to a lab or creating a home lab where you can safely play with the technologies. Searching the internet for *home security lab* will locate a variety of options, from laptop-based labs to a full server-based setup. Perhaps you could create it in the cloud. Cost and time will be a factor. Use your lab to learn about Active Directory, running DNS and DHCP, network zones, firewalls, Kali Linux, and various operating systems.

Technical skills can also take the form of governance, risk, and compliance (GRC). This is about using technical knowledge to create and apply frameworks, regulations, and oversight to an organization. It might include auditing and other assessment functions. Sometimes, people also include security architecture in the GRC field. People in GRC tend to start by knowing one or two technologies and quickly learn how to apply these to business processes and other nontechnology disciplines.

It is impossible to know everything about all the technologies. Do the things you like to do. There are hot jobs out there right now — cloud security, IoT, data analytics, artificial intelligence, and so on — but any technology is a place to start, and those skills will help you transfer later into any number of security roles. Check out books like these:

- *The Pentester Blueprint: Starting a Career as an Ethical Hacker* by Phillip L. Wylie and Kim Crawley
- *Confident Cyber Security: How To Get Started in Cyber Security and Future Proof Your Career* by Dr. Jessica Barker.

Also, check out these blogs:

- Leslie Carhart, Starting an Infosec Career (https://tisiphone.net/2015/10/12/starting-an-infosec-career-the-megamix-chapters-1-3/)
- Daniel Miessler, How to Build a Cybersecurity Career (https://danielmiessler.com/blog/build-successful-infosec-career/

Regardless of where you focus, I suggest you focus on that area for at least a couple of years. (This also depends on your industry. Two years in a start-up company is a long time, though it's not very long in financial services.) It's impossible to know everything about all technology layers. A general understanding of the technology layers and how they relate, combined with at least a couple of years of focus on one type of technology, will provide a solid foundation for almost any security job. This is why many people start in traditional IT fields (networking, help desk, or application development) and then move over into a security function after that. If you're not already in a technology field, consider making that kind of move as a potential first step.

Professional Skills

While you work on your technology skills, what else do you need? For this, stay away from job descriptions. The requirements are so vague (usually) that they're meaningless, such as excellent communication skills, strong organizational skills, and teamwork. Security leaders will tell you they can teach you the technology skills, but teaching "soft" skills is a lot of effort. It's interesting that most job descriptions focus on the technical but not the "soft skills."

There is nothing "soft" about being an employee who can communicate well, who can collaborate across organizational boundaries, or who can make difficult decisions based on strong analysis. Instead, call them *professional skills*. They are required to be a security professional, and I've never met a successful security person who lacks professional skills. I've met plenty of technology wizards who lack professional skills and who are awful at security. Just like technology skills, you never stop improving your professional skills. As a person looking for their first job in the security field, you need to find ways to show recruiters and hiring managers what your professional skills are. Also, you should know that we are all learning as we go. In Figure 5.2, you can see how one colleague approached improving her professional skills and the factors she considered.

While you're working on building up your technology portfolio, work on the skills discussed in the following sections, too.

Communication Skills

Communication skills fall into two categories: writing and talking.

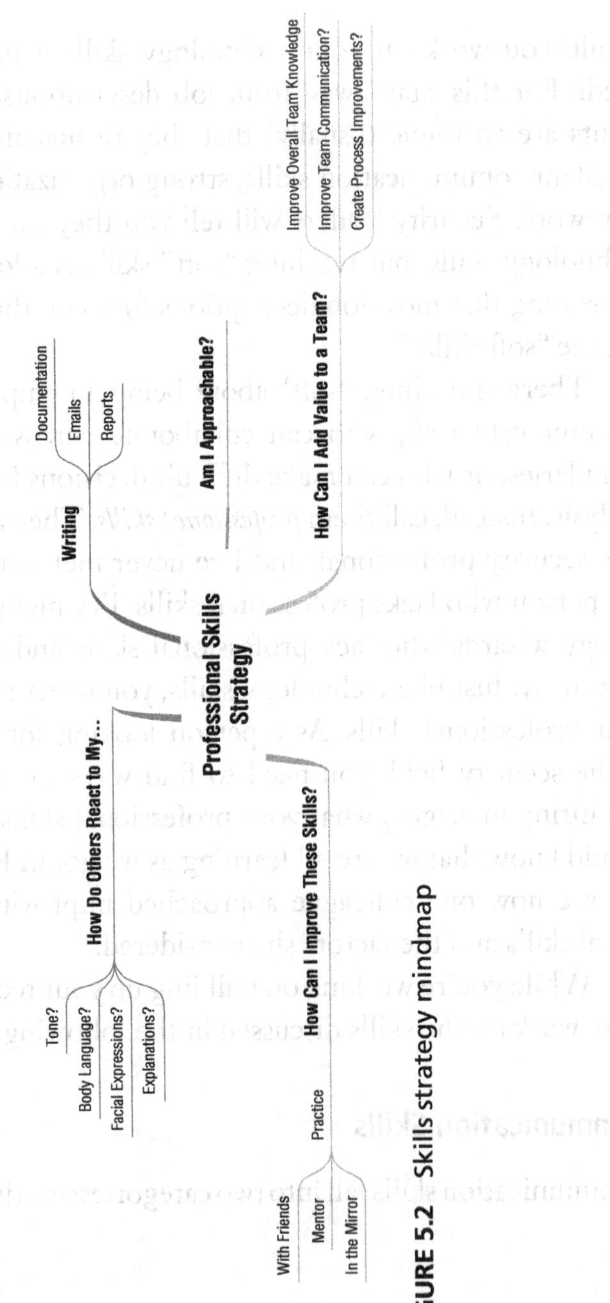

FIGURE 5.2 Skills strategy mindmap

In the beginning, when we talked about security writing skills, we meant technical writing. Later, it also came to mean "being able to write so nontechnical executives can understand our message." A long, flowery essay can be beautiful and serves lots of good business purposes, though such an essay might obscure the facts at a time when you need to be crisp and to the point.

Working in security means being able to answer management questions succinctly. It means anticipating what those questions are, using data to support your answer, and writing your reports and papers so that those questions are answered quickly. Know what the business case is and how to write it. The structures of business cases support making a reasoned, articulate argument and are familiar to most business leaders.

If you've never taken a technical writing class, consider doing it. Your security writing will include process documentation, analysis papers, or operational reports. These require technical writing skills, so find someone who does it well and make a mentor out of that person.

You will also do a lot of communication by email or chat channels. Know the protocols for writing email/chats that get your point across as effectively as possible. If you struggle with writing, learn to use the tools that help you check for spelling and grammar. Avail yourself of proofreaders for important pieces. I cannot overstate how important this skill is to master — even for the most junior positions.

Talking skills involve communicating with and presenting to others.

> Being able to get your point across clearly and concisely is a required skill in many professions, particularly security.

Making presentations and persuading people are part of every security person's job. As a junior person, your presentations skills might be focused on small groups. As you progress, you will present to management and other stakeholders. Later, you might present to large teams or conference audiences. It is never too early to learn how to give a presentation at a conference. Even as a junior person, this is a great way to network! If you're not comfortable speaking in formal situations, there are plenty of public-speaking classes (such as Toastmasters) available — use them. Practice speaking in front of a mirror. Record yourself speaking and judge yourself critically. When you're ready, present to other people who will give you constructive criticism — and be ready to take it!

Your résumé is the first place people will assess your writing skills, so make sure you ask other people to proofread your résumé before you send it anywhere. Cover letters are a great way to highlight your writing skills, but make sure they are done well. Ask others to critique your cover letter before you include it with an application. Nothing undermines you faster than saying you have "superior writing skills" when your résumé has typos! Providing samples of writing (redacting any sensitive information) during interviews can be helpful. Listing speaking engagements on a résumé is also great. Even better, if your presentation was recorded live, provide a link to your presentation.

Emotional Intelligence

I once had a boss tell me, "You might be right, but you're not being effective." This piece of coaching stung, but it was the pivotal feedback that took me from being a so-so manager to a security leader. And it took a *lot* of work to learn how to be effective, not just correct. You will know when you bump into someone with a low emotional intelligence (EI), also known as emotional quotient (EQ). People with low EI create unnecessary drama, cause lots of misunderstandings, and are perceived as being stubborn or conceited. It takes them longer to get things done, and other people don't like working with them. Make sure this isn't you! The irony is that folks with low EI don't know that they have low EI and often think they have high EI. Consider reading *Emotional Intelligence* by Daniel Goleman to learn more. Emotional intelligence isn't something to put directly on a résumé. Your EI shows up positively when other people want to act as a reference (providing testimonials on LinkedIn, for example), you deliver initiatives on time, or you are a mentor for other people. If you must explicitly state that you have emotional intelligence, you probably don't. In Goleman's book, he notes five characteristics of emotional intelligence, which are outlined in the following table:

Daniel Goleman's Emotional Intelligence

Element	Description
Emotional self-awareness	Knowing what you're feeling and how that impacts others
Self-regulation	Anticipating, controlling, and redirecting emotions
Motivation	Using emotion to achieve goals
Empathy	Sensing others' emotions
Social skills	Relationship management and inspiring others

Effective Listening

To have emotional intelligence, communicate effectively, and form strong partnerships, you must be skilled at listening effectively.

You must learn how to listen to others to know their stated and unstated needs and motivations and then reflect them.

Know your own triggers: what gets you excited, what gets you stressed, and how you behave when that happens. You need to know when to push and when to back away. There are resources to help you, starting by talking to family, teammates, and others. Ask them what they observe about you. Consider reading *Crucial Conversations: Tools for Talking When The Stakes Are High* by Patterson, Grenny, McMillan, and Switzler. Be prepared to take feedback from them graciously. It will be worth your time.

Partnership

Related to emotional intelligence, partnership is also a necessary skill to learn. Hiring managers call it "teamwork," but it's more than just getting along with the rest of your immediate team. It's also the ability to work across and beyond the entire organization to achieve goals that couldn't be done alone. It's about intentionally cultivating personal relationships with key partners so you have mutual trust during difficult conversations. It's taking time to meet with people just to learn more about who they are, without any expectation of transactional benefit.

If you are a great partner, you are infinitely more effective than someone who just "does their job." You look for ways to improve processes that cut across multiple teams. You take time to understand why other people and teams do things in a particular way. You try to see the world from their perspective, not just your own. Conversely, people with awful partnership skills damage the entire team and take more emotional/managerial effort than they are worth. These are the people no one likes to work with, others will actively try to work around, and no one trusts.

Again, testimonials on LinkedIn or hiring references are a nice way to demonstrate your partnership skills. References are useful, too.

Initiative

Things change in security all the time. There will never be a time in your career that you know all you need to know or that you've done all you need to do. Hiring managers expect you to be a self-starter. They expect you will continue to challenge yourself to learn new things, from technology skills to learning more about how the business works. These might be things related to your job, and they might also be new things to learn "just because you can." They expect that even if you're a junior employee, you'll look for ways to improve how your job works, how the organization works, and how the organization's security profile can be improved.

How do you show initiative on a résumé or in an interview? Explicitly list work or activities where you took the initiative to do something. Use verbs. For example, saying "attended boot camp," "presented at a conference," or "self-taught this security skill" all go to showing that the hiring manager won't have to prod you to take on new skills or tasks.

When you are applying for a security job, it is highly unlikely that you will have all the skills the hiring manager is looking for. (And if you did, would you really want the job anyway?) Look for a job with a company you'd like to work for, with the work conditions you hope to have, where you have some of the skills they want, and where you can grow. And go from there.

What's Next?

- Check out some job postings for the kind of security job you want. Note the kind of skills they require or the optional ones. (Also, check out the "Resources" appendix.) Make a note of the common skills/traits.
- Practice presenting security ideas to others. Get feedback and take constructive criticism as the gift it is.
- Talk to people you work with or who know you, and ask them to share what they think your personal strengths and opportunities are. Encourage them to be completely honest.
- Do a personal skills inventory. Note your technical and social/emotional strengths. Note the skills you are missing (compared to the job postings you checked out) or that are weak.
- Consider whether your strengths align with the kind of security jobs you want. If so, great! If not, you can choose to work on the skills you need or consider a different security career path.

CHAPTER

6

Is My Résumé Okay?

Summary

- **Sell yourself:** Make sure your résumé is tailored to a particular company and for a particular job; it should not be generic. Include all relevant educational experience and any hobbies that might indicate an affinity for security.
- **Sell yourself more:** Always — always — include a cover letter, and use it to explain things that can't be included on your résumé. Use your résumé to show what you know and what your potential is.
- **Sell yourself all the time:** Make sure you have an up-to-date profile on LinkedIn or other social media.

Once you have determined what kind of role you want, the skills and experience that are required, and where you want to apply, you then have to create a résumé. The résumé needs to be specific enough to get past the computer recruiting algorithms that will filter candidates who lack matching skills. It needs to be creative enough to catch the eye of the recruiter and hiring manager as they sift through many similar candidates. It needs to show all the skills and experience you have, without over- or understating your qualifications. Lastly, it needs to give the hiring manager a sense of who you are. No wonder job seekers get stressed about writing a résumé!

Many new job seekers think a résumé is something like a school transcript. It shows the work you have already done and the skills you have already learned. People know they don't have all the skills the hiring manager is asking for, so they struggle to know if they have included the right things. Seekers might not lie, but they get as creative as possible with their wording to try to impress the hiring manager. As a result, beginner résumés tend to be self-focused and past tense. What did I do? What did I learn? How did I advance? What was I interested in? What did I want? If you think a résumé exists to help a manager learn about you, you make the résumé all about the things you have done.

Reveal your potential, not just your history.

As you progress through your career, you realize that your résumé should not just be a look back at your history. It is also meant to be a guide to your future. A good résumé doesn't just say "this is what I have done." It also says "this is what I *can* do." So, create your résumé to talk about you and talk about the impact you have on other people and companies. Instead of saying "participated in an internship," focus on how you helped the company by saying "worked on XY project that resulted in enhanced awareness training for X thousand employees." Highlight the self-taught learning you have done, the technical papers you have written, and the "so what" of that effort. If you're a little more experienced, talk about the people you have mentored and the presentations you have given to the security community.

Résumés are tricky things. For entry-level people, the challenge with a résumé is that you don't have lots of skills and experience. You're trying to creatively include nonprofessional things to signal the kind of employee you want to be (but are not — yet). As you spend more time in the workforce, the challenge becomes deciding what to include (or not include) and making sure your résumé is accurate and reflects what you've done and what you want to do.

A good résumé is one that concisely gives the background of an individual and reveals their "why." It's terrific when it connects to the advertised role, shows an awareness of the industry and the type of position, and most importantly gives a sense of who the candidate is.

A bad résumé is one that seems like it is written without regard for the advertised position or the hiring company. It is awful if it reveals a lack of care or inattention to detail. It's really awful when it is unstructured, unplanned, and without purpose.

It is often overlooked that the purpose of a résumé is to make it easier for hiring managers and recruiters to identify potential candidates and more quickly winnow out of the hiring pool anyone who might be less suitable. In other words, the résumé isn't for you, the candidate. Instead, it's for the hiring manager. So, how do you write a meaningful résumé if you don't even know who the hiring manager is or exactly what they are looking for?

Whether you are just starting out or considering your next move, there are some common items to consider when preparing a security résumé, as you'll see shortly in the following sections.

Linking the Résumé to the Job Posting

Some people have one standard résumé that they use for every job posting. They leave any customization to the cover letter. This strategy misses the opportunity to really stand out from other candidates.

> Have a "standard" résumé, but make sure you tweak it for each job application. It shows that you care about not just the job but the company itself, which goes a long way toward making your résumé stand out from the crowd.

Writing a superior résumé means doing your homework on the company, the hiring manager, the industry, and the role itself.

- What industry is the company in? Is it a highly regulated one? Is it a new industry? Is the industry established or struggling? Why would you want to work in this kind of industry?
- What is the mission of this company? What do they care about? Profits? Community? Innovation? Why would you want to work in this kind of company?
- Who is the hiring manager? What is their background? Are they a technologist or a compliance officer? First-time manager? Forming a new team? Running a long-running team? Why would you want to work for this manager?
- What is the role? Is it one of many roles at the company? Is it a new role for the company? Is the person who did the role still there? (Perhaps they are the hiring manager and are hiring their replacement.) Why are you applying for this role?

You might not be able to get all these questions answered, but you should try to get as many answers as you can before writing your résumé and cover letter. You're trying to determine what the company and the hiring manager value. An internet search is a great way to get a lot of this. Networking and talking to folks from the target company are always useful. If you know the answers, you can then work out whether this role is good for you. You can determine whether it's worth chasing in the first place. If you think it is worth pursuing, then this information can be used to tune your résumé to align with the things they value. It lets you know what skills to put at the top of the page and what to list later (if at all). It helps you know what keywords to include (not just for résumé filters but also for those who read your résumé).

Sometimes you're trying to find any role, and you're playing a numbers game. The more résumés you send out, the more chances of landing a job, any job. Especially in the beginning, for common entry-level roles, this is okay. This might be all you have time to do. In this case, you are looking to create a generic résumé by role. For example, if you're looking for an entry-level SOC analyst role, you would just key your experience to a generic SOC analyst position without layering on the manager/company/industry elements. You would hope that you hit enough generic points to land an interview. Once you get the interview, you can then spend time doing the background research. This is a perfectly good strategy; just know that you will need to send out a lot more résumés to get an interview, so be prepared for this outcome.

Elements of a Résumé

When a hiring manager picks up a résumé, they are expecting to see some standard sections and information, so be prepared to give it to them. The exact order and detail will vary based on you and the role you're applying for, but ultimately, most résumés have the same kind of details.

Header and Summary

You would think it would be straightforward: name, address, and so on. Well, this is a security résumé, so think again. Name? Fine. Address? No. Don't include a full physical address, because it's not relevant, and it might be the basis of immediate elimination. Maybe a city and state name are okay if you really feel that you need to share a location. Include an email address and a phone number. (Please be careful of the appropriateness of the email name; keep it plain and boring!) You might also include a link to LinkedIn or a personal website if you are so inclined.

Some people like to include a summary statement. I love reading summary statements — because it's really the only place on a résumé where you can be overt about why you're applying for this job. Make sure your summary statement aligns with the job and company for which you are applying. Otherwise, you will immediately cut yourself from the candidate pool. Make the summary cover the job you're pursuing *now*; it should not cover your aspirational career goals. Again, remember that you're writing this for the hiring manager, not for you. Help them know why you are the right candidate for this job right now.

Work Experience

Security hiring managers tend to value experience over formal education, so start with job experience first. If you have a continuous chronological job history using the traditional résumé format of listing your jobs in reverse chronological order (most recent job first), this is great. If you don't have a continuous job history, listing jobs without detailing exact chronology can also work. If you're a student entering the workforce for the first time, this will be expected and accepted. If you've been in the workforce for a few years and don't offer a chronological view, be prepared to address this in your cover letter and interviews.

Here's the thing about listing jobs on your résumé: titles are meaningless. A "security analyst" can mean thousands of different things, as can "security engineer." Even more targeted titles such as "vulnerability engineer" can mean different things depending on how an individual company does "vulnerability management." So, when you're listing your work history, you must give context, not just the company/title/dates. Describe what you did in that role, what skills/technologies you used, how you helped the business, and what skills you mastered. Use verbs (action words) to describe your work. For example, say "managed 20,000 endpoints," "analyzed third-party applications," or "executed 50 penetration tests."

Don't forget to include the outcome of your work — the "so what." It's good to say that you "managed 20,000 endpoints," but it's better if you can show why that was good or useful. For example, you could instead say "managed 20,000 endpoints and remediated 150,000 vulnerabilities in 3 months" or "reduced high-risk vulnerabilities by 20 percent."

Skills

My preference is to incorporate skills into the work experience section because it helps tell your "this is what I did, and this is what I learned" story. Some people prefer to have skills in a separate section. Either way, make sure you link the skills you are listing to the kind of job you are seeking. Put the most relevant skills high up on the list so they stand out to the hiring manager. Focus on any "required skills" from the job posting. Do this even if they are not your strongest skills. Make the hiring manager notice that you have what they need. Add in any "preferred skills" next, and then add any other security or complementary skills to round out your background.

If you are going to list technical skills, be careful not to oversell or undersell yourself. If you are calling yourself an "expert" when you've been working on the skill for less than two years, you're lying. If you say you are "learning" when you have five years working on that technology, you are either too humble or a really bad learner. Be accurate!

When you think of skills, it's easy to think about the technology skills and forget about professional (or "soft") skills. Don't. Hiring managers are looking for people who can write well, know how to present, and are great team players. Don't overlook including these skills in your résumé. Here are some examples:

- Worked with a team of five to manage third-party application assessments, resulting in a 30 percent reduction in known risk
- Presented the application security strategy to senior leaders, who approved the requested budget
- Identified process improvements for the access management team, resulting in a 20 percent time-efficiency saving

Some people worry if they don't have all the skills listed in the job posting and will apply only if they meet all the required skills. While you want to have some of the skills, don't stress if you don't have all of them. (What would be the point of doing a job you already fully know?). Most hiring managers don't spend a lot of time making the job posting completely accurate for the job that will ultimately be done. Instead, they list the skills to make sure you're in the ballpark, so if you have only 60 percent of the skills and it's a job you want, apply anyway.

Education

As a hiring manager, the first thing I look at in the education section is the dates. Dates tell me how recently the candidate took training and whether the candidate continues to invest in themselves, so don't think of education as only formal education. Sure, you should include any college degrees you have, but you should also include professional training, boot camps, self-learning, professional certificates, and conference attendance.

Most hiring managers will not care about your GPA or other scores. The only exception to this might be a college student with no other work experience, so err on the side of *not* including your GPA or other exam scores. Although if you want to brag about an honors or cum laude result, go right ahead. Certainly, don't include the scores if they are middle or low!

Do *not* be vague about certifications. If you have a certification and it's active, great! If you've taken a certification exam but are not yet fully certified, then explicitly say that (for example, "Completed coursework in pursuit of an XYZ certification"). If you used to have a certification but it's lapsed, then say that, too. I've seen more than one employee be fired for lying about their certifications or education status on their résumé. Don't be that person.

Extra Curricula Things

Your "hobbies" are a great way to help hiring managers find reasons to look closely at your candidacy. The hiring manager is going to be looking for evidence that you are interested in security for its own sake, particularly if this is your first security job, regardless of whether you're going for an entry-level position or sliding into a lateral role from another discipline. When you're putting your résumé and cover letter together, don't forget to mention the out-of-band things you do that might show your interest, such as the following:

- Membership in a cyber club or professional organization
- If you have a Kali/Linux server that you play around with
- Participation in capture-the-flag (CTF) events or other training
- Security conference attendance

There are other, less obvious hobbies that will stand out to a security hiring manager. Interest in puzzles and board games, lockpicking, ham radio operations, participation in escape room activities, and anything to do with emergency management or disaster response are some of the indicators of a way of thinking that are valued by the security community.

Landing a security job will take more than professional education or certifications, so make sure you showcase your interest.

Keywords and Ways to Get Noticed

Your résumé has to help you get noticed to land an interview. If you're not getting interviews, the problem might be your résumé.

Many times, the hiring manager isn't the first person to see your résumé or select you for an interview. It's a recruiter (or algorithm) who knows nothing (usually) about security. You must be careful about your choice of words and to make sure your résumé includes keywords that will be noticed by recruiters and algorithms. This is where specifically linking your résumé to the job you're seeking comes in handy. Look at the job posting, and make sure your résumé has the same words (as close to exactly as you can get). For example, if they're looking for a "project manager," then don't put "managing projects" in your résumé. Find a way to put "project manager" there instead. If the company values "customer experience," then try to find a way to put "customer experience" into your résumé.

Keywords are particularly useful to check for certifications. If you have studied for a certification, even if you have not yet passed the test or if the certification has lapsed, make sure you include it on your résumé so the keyword matching finds you.

For our ex-military or government friends: if you have a security clearance, or even a lapsed clearance, list it on your résumé. Even if the job doesn't require a security clearance, it is a coveted feature for security team members and will be positively received by the hiring manager.

Once you have created your résumé, ask someone (preferably a security manager) to give you feedback on it. They can help you refine it to put a sharper spotlight on relevant skills and experiences. When you ask someone to review your résumé, make sure you also give them the job posting for which you're applying. This will help them help you make the résumé relevant.

Digital Presence

In the same way an artist compiles a portfolio of work, so can a security professional compile a digital portfolio that can be reviewed by prospective hiring managers.

- Start with a LinkedIn page. In addition to detailing work experience, it can show your relationships to professional organizations. Also, it can show you topical posts about security issues and how you're networked to the security community. If you're going to have a LinkedIn page, make sure you're active on it. This doesn't mean you have to write your own posts (although that would be good, too!). However, reading other posts and commenting or "liking" things you see shows active mental engagement in the security community.

- If you're into software development, including a GitHub repository can demonstrate your coding skills.
- Consider blogging. Even as someone new to security, maintaining a blog can show prospective employers that you're interested in security, you're learning about security topics, and, most importantly, you know how to write!
- Personal websites can be a good thing, too. A simple site that shows what you've been working on (maintaining the confidentiality of the companies you are helping, of course), classes you've taken, certifications you've acquired, and so on can be useful to a hiring manager.

References

Before you begin a job search, make sure you have two or three references lined up who are willing to advocate for your skills and experience. If your references are from the target company or you know people in the target company who can advocate on your behalf, then that's a bonus.

If you have no job experience, find references who know you and can attest to your character. Are you honest, hardworking, and curious? Teachers and mentors are great for this, but family and friends will also be helpful if you are just starting out.

You don't need to list references on your résumé! It used to be customary to include them or minimally note that "references are available upon request." These days, it is not necessary to include this. The space on your résumé is better used for other things. If you get to an interview, you can bring copies of your references with you or at least mention that you have references available.

Cover Letters

Every time you submit a job application, include a cover letter. The cover letter gives you the opportunity to be more detailed about the specific job you're applying for, why you're excited about the role, and why they should hire you.

Take the opportunity to get the exact company name, contact names, and job titles correct. If you can, avoid using "To whom it may concern" or "Dear Sir/Madam" for salutations. Focus their attention on the relevant parts of your résumé, such as, "As you can see by my education regarding X, I am very interested in your position . . ."

Make sure the tone of your cover letter matches the hiring company. Use your knowledge of their mission/vision/values to know how they communicate. If they are formal, make your cover letter formal. If they are casual, your cover letter can be, too. Be upbeat. This is your chance to show enthusiasm for both working in security and doing *this* job for *this* company.

If there are gaps in your résumé, the cover letter is the place to call that out at a high level. An obvious gap in work history, a particularly long time to complete a degree, or other flags on your résumé can be addressed here. You don't have to go deep. Just acknowledge the gap exists, give a brief explanation why ("the company I worked for declared bankruptcy" or "I worked full time while completing my degree"), and let them know you would be happy to discuss further.

Use the cover letter to help them work with you. Give them your detailed contact information and available times to meet. Make it as easy as possible to work with you. If you know someone who works at the company, mention it in your cover letter. (Make sure that person knows you are doing it and is okay with it!)

As always, get someone to proofread your cover letter!

What's Next?

- Create a generic security résumé for each type of job you hope to land.
- Create a cover letter template that is ready to be modified for each job.
- Update your LinkedIn profile. Make sure you're using it to actively engage with the security community and topics.
- Consider other social media or online options and begin participating in those activities.
- Share your draft résumé and social media profiles with security contacts and managers. Ask them for feedback and incorporate that into your résumé and online presence.
- If you're ready to start using your résumé to search for jobs, prepare your references.

CHAPTER

7

Trying with Little Success?

Summary

- **Know your audience:** Learn about the locations, industries, and companies you are applying to. Understand what kind of business they are in and what kind of security person they need.
- **Know yourself:** Determine if your problem is in landing interviews or landing jobs. The solution to the problem will be different. It might be your résumé

needs improvement, or it's your interviewing skills that need work. Get feedback on both.

- **Network:** Stay active in the security community and get noticed online. People want to help you!

Some people searching for a security role run into roadblocks. Perhaps they can't find companies they want to work for. Perhaps they can find the right company, but that company isn't hiring the kind of jobs they want to take. Perhaps the job on offer is in the wrong location. Perhaps they are applying for roles, but they don't hear back. Even knowing there is an oversupply of security jobs and an undersupply of labor, it can feel like a challenge to look for and land a security job.

This is true whether you are looking for your first security job or your tenth. Even CISOs looking for a new role find it difficult. In fact, the more senior the role, the longer it takes to find it. Even though I've been in the security profession for a couple of decades, looking for and landing a new security job is a challenge, and it will be a challenge for you, too.

Don't give up! Persistence is required. Constantly evaluating yourself, your environment, the hiring processes, and the hiring communities will also help you find your security role. There is a place for you. Give yourself the time and grace to find it.

Know that it is rarely about you.

Despite the widespread reports of lots of jobs being available, there are a number of factors that make *your* job search and the opportunities available to you unique. Your job search is influenced by the following:

- Where you live
- What companies are around you
- What kind of industries they represent
- How they are regulated
- Who else is competing for your jobs
- What kind of skills and experience you have

We've been led to believe that the need for security talent is so great that we should be able to show up, demonstrate interest, and land a job. Well, no one has told hiring managers that. Hiring managers are still looking for the skills, experience, and "fit" that they always have, and they are not as willing as they should be to look outside the usual places for new talent. Until this changes, you should expect that job searches will take time and will be competitive.

Hiring managers are almost never taught how to hire. Few managers are taught how to write a job description, let alone a job posting. Recruiters rarely understand how security roles are created or what a hiring manager truly looks for in a candidate. Companies use search platforms that don't allow for nuance, which filters out valid candidates (you). This results in job postings that are not clear about what they expect or have requirements that are impossible to meet.

If you have been trying to land an interview or are trying to conclude an interview with a job, the following sections include some things to think about.

My Story

I choose to live in Columbus, Ohio. Columbus is one of the best-kept secrets in the United States — a technology hub and the home of several Fortune 100 companies. Columbus sports a diversity of industries and people, provides a low cost of living, and is a great place to raise a family. It's close to many major U.S. cities, has a world-class university right in the middle of the city, and so on.

Despite this — and even knowing there is an oversupply of security jobs and an undersupply of labor — it can feel like a challenge to look for and land a security job. Why? Well, when I search for security jobs, the companies hiring the most are usually situated on the East or West coasts. If I were sitting in Silicon Valley, New York, or DC, there would be a lot more options. Also, even though there are a lot of companies with a Columbus presence, many of them are headquartered elsewhere, and the internal security team is typically located there. This means that even with more people working remotely, the ability to find a security job where I'm part of a team is more limited, and the competition for those jobs is higher.

The more senior the job, the longer the looking/interviewing/hiring process takes. Hiring managers are paying more for senior talent, so the hiring process is more complex — with more interviews and more conversations. For any one opportunity I pursue, I expect the process to take upward of six months to complete. Moving around takes time and energy. Persistence is great, but constantly evaluating yourself, your environment, and the hiring processes will help you find your security role.

Physical Location

As with any job search, knowing the field of play is extremely important. If you're based in a big city or in a technology hub, the general opportunities are much better than someone in a smaller city or country town. If you aren't surrounded by mass opportunity, you need to think about how you're willing to engage with potential employers. Are you willing to relocate? Are you willing to travel a lot, even if you don't leave your home base? Are you willing to work remotely 100 percent of the time? If you are posting for your first security job, I recommend looking for a role where you are actively engaged with teammates so you can learn quickly. Being remote is great, but it's usually better for people with some experience who can work independently. If you are going to be remote, make sure the company you choose has a strong track record in hiring and developing remote workers. If you're having trouble landing a role, consider expanding the location of your search to widen the pool of opportunity.

Some candidates choose to make location restrictions clear on their cover letter, in any communications they share with hiring teams, and so on. Others wait until they are asked in for an interview and/or are close to receiving a job offer before discussing location. I prefer to be up front about my location requirements, even though this might make me lose out on interviews or offers. If you've been overt about your location and you are not receiving any interviews or callbacks, try keeping this information close until you are further down the hiring path.

Your Company

If you are already working in a larger company in a nonsecurity role, consider whether your company might offer a chance to move into a security role internally. This is often a faster path than trying to break into a security role in a new company. Look for tasks/projects that offer security experience and shoot for those. Start working on security things where you are and then find ways to partner more closely with the security team.

For example, if you are a project manager, ask for assignments that include a security component. (Or take it upon yourself to engage the security team as part of the project; they will love you!) If you are a software developer, find ways to test your code on the job or learn more about the testing tools (or implement testing tools). The security teams can't be everywhere all the time, and they *love* nonsecurity people who find ways to initiate good security practices outside their own teams. This combination of showing initiative and partnering with the security team will set you up to be considered (or even invited) for a new security role when one becomes available.

Even if you are in a company without a security team, it can be a career boost to purposefully do security work where you are and then reference this work on a résumé when looking for a job with another company. Use online or network partners to help you get started. Most long-time security people got started in security because no one else in their company was doing it, and they just jumped in. This can be you, too.

Get Specific

Often, I have someone who asks me questions about getting a "security job." That's a great place to start a conversation, but not specific enough to allow them to easily find a suitable role.

Security is a sprawling and complex field. If you want hiring managers to notice you or mentors to help you, you must have a general idea about the different security roles and which type of role you want to pursue. You don't have to be super-specific. Even a general class of roles is a great place to start, such as training and awareness, vulnerability management, application security, risk and governance, and the like.

If you are sending out lots of résumés and getting no response, it might be because your résumé is too general and not well aligned to the roles for which you are applying. Consider sharpening your résumé to be specific to a certain type of security role. Look at the words you use, and the experience you highlight, the skills you mention, and make sure they are as closely aligned to that specific security job as possible.

If you are getting called in for interviews but not receiving an offer, it might be because you're not articulating why *this* role is the one you want. Make sure you know what you want and why and target your résumés and interview answers accordingly. Be prepared to talk to the screeners and the interviewers about why this job is appealing to you. Use your cover letter to express your excitement about this kind of work. If you can, highlight the projects and training you've done for this kind of job.

If you're already in a nonsecurity job and trying to move over into a security role, be clear about whether you are willing to move into a more junior security role in order to make the change. Sometimes, you must take a lateral or downward move to find a security job, knowing that you will likely quickly rise up again because of your other experience. But not all people can afford to take a pay cut to move over. Are you willing to do this? This isn't something to put on a résumé or cover letter. But when you're talking to people, if you feel the role you're applying for is more junior than your current one, be direct about your willingness to be considered. Hiring managers are reluctant to hire someone they consider to be overqualified or too senior, so you will need to convince them that you're comfortable taking this path.

Know Your Market

Just as a good marketer will learn about their potential clients, a job seeker should learn about the opportunities in the target market. Review local business publications/websites to see what kinds of companies are in your pool of potential employers. Know what kind of industries they are in, whether they are growing, and what kind of security jobs they are looking to hire.

If your target is anywhere in the country, reading about the security industry in general or even security industry reports like the Verizon Data Breach Investigations Report can help you understand who is looking for talent and what kind of talent they are seeking.

You might find that you've been applying for jobs in companies whose industries are in a recession. These companies are looking for someone who can start adding value immediately (with less tolerance for "teaching on the job"). You might be applying for roles requiring common skills, so the number of applicants is higher than normal, which creates competition. If you have been focusing your job applications in a certain industry with no response, consider trying a different industry. Consider trying a different position if you've been focusing on a certain type of role with no response.

If you've been getting interviews but not job offers, consider brushing up on the business of your target company before you speak to a recruiter or hiring manager so you know what kind of industry pressures are influencing their thinking. Is the company a high-volume, low-margin business? Maybe the company has only a few high-wealth customers? What is their company vision and mission? Are they active in the community or keeping to themselves? Knowing the answers to these questions and incorporating them into your résumé, cover letter, and conversations will help distinguish you from other candidates.

Don't forget to take a look at their culture! Before talking to anyone, make sure you know their values and find ways to incorporate those values into your discussions or presentations. For example, if the company is in a heavily regulated industry, find out what regulations apply (HIPAA, PCI, NERC-CIP, and so on) and reference those regulations when you speak. If they care about diversity, inclusion, and equity, reflect that in your conversations.

Assess Your Efforts So Far

Job seekers tend to fall into two categories: either they are not getting any phone screens or interviews at all, or they get interviews that don't result in job offers. These are two different problems with potentially different solutions.

If your problem is that you're not getting called for phone screens or interviews, spend some time focusing on your résumé and internet presence. Ask a mentor or senior advisor to review your résumé and LinkedIn profile, and ask for pointers. In general, make sure that:

- Your résumé focuses on the type of job you're applying for and isn't just a generalist résumé.
- You highlight any security skills and experience that are relevant for the job, and it is not just a regurgitation of all your experience, ever.
- You include any extracurricular activities you do that are related to security. This includes participation in networking groups, conferences, public speaking, volunteering, and the like.

- You include a cover letter that explains your "why" — why security, why this company, and why this role.
- Your social media file shows active engagement with the security community. Make sure to show that you're part of security groups, you are connected to security people (bonus if they are people in your target companies), and you are commenting (appropriately) on security-related posts.

If your problem is that you are getting called by recruiters but not landing an interview, consider practicing your phone skills and marketing pitch. Take time to think about the kind of questions a recruiter/screener might ask. Practice mock phone screens with a friend, colleague, or mentor. Review any email exchanges you have had to identify opportunities to sell yourself better. Take feedback graciously and make changes.

If your problem is that you get interviews but no job offers, it's time to take a look at your interviewing skills. Again, work with a mentor/coach/colleague to practice mock interviews. If possible, ask target companies if they will let you do "information interviews" where you interview *them*. This is a great way for them to get to know you, and you can practice your skills in a low-stress way. At the end of an interview, it's completely appropriate to ask the interviewer if they have any reservations about hiring you. During the interview, always ask the interviewer for feedback. Do they have any more questions or concerns about your background/experience that you can answer? Do they see any gaps/weaknesses in your candidacy that you can address while you are there? They will often give you their "first impression" response, which might not be accurate, but it will let you know how you're showing up in the interview.

Pay attention to your appearance. As much as I hate that appearance counts, it does. Know the dress code of the companies where you are interviewing, and do your best to be slightly more formal for an interview. Wearing a suit to a tech start-up interview is probably overkill, but dressing in "business-slightly-formal" clothing is great. Wearing business-informal clothing to a financial firm is under-dressed and will signal that you aren't prepared for the role.

Consider working with a security recruiting firm. They can help you sharpen up all your job-seeking skills and know when jobs are becoming available. Some security staffing firms will place you in temporary contract roles, some of which will be temporary-to-hire. This might be a way to get known, add more experience, and potentially get hired, all at the same time.

But I'm Doing All Those Things!

If all the previous suggestions are already known to you, here are some reminders:

- Don't underestimate the power of networking. I've mentioned this extensively in the rest of the book, and I will reinforce it here, too. You must be getting out into the security community in any way you can. The community will both help you with your search and be a positive support system while you're searching. This could include volunteering with local security organizations.
- Promote yourself. Don't just rely on networking. Find a way to be visible in the community. Volunteer at your local security professional chapters, give security-related presentations at work or your local school, post to a blog, and so on. And promote those things on your social media accounts.
- Remember that this is a numbers game. Sending out only a few résumés will be a slow process. The more jobs you apply

for, even if you don't feel fully qualified for them, the more you might find.

- Consider pivoting into security, rather than using a direct approach. That means finding an adjacent role (help desk, systems administration, application development, or compliance) and do security tasks within that job. Use that learning to move to a security role later.

I hope these suggestions are helpful to you. Good luck!

What's Next?

- Evaluate what's going on. Is it your résumé? Your phone interviewing skills? Your in-person skills? Or something else entirely?
- If you haven't already done it, have someone review your cover letter and résumé. Conduct mock phone and in-person interviews.
- Reach out to your network to get advice on how to address your problem areas.
- It might not be you! Consider looking in different places for the job you want — a different industry, location, or function.
- While you're waiting for the job to appear, do what you can to continue your training.

PART

II

Thriving in Security

Congratulations, you are a security professional!

People are so excited when they finally land a security position — any position — and they dive right into the new role. After a while, the honeymoon is over, they have stopped drinking from the fire hose, and they now have time to stick their head up and look around. When they do, they notice that working in security has many blessings and many challenges.

Many of their questions apply to any kind of job, in any profession. Issues of manager/employee interactions, career advancement, glass ceilings, and balancing family and professional life are not limited to the security domain. The questions I answer in this part have a specific security flavor. There is something about working in security that makes the problem harder to navigate or more complicated. In this part, we cover the following topics:

Chapter 8, "How Do I Keep Up?"

In this chapter, we talk about how security and technology keep changing and how to deal with those changes.

Chapter 9, "How Can I Manage Security Stress?"

In this chapter, we examine what makes working in security stressful and how to address the root causes of security stress.

Chapter 10, "How Can I Succeed As A Minority?"

The security profession isn't particularly diverse. In this chapter, we talk about coping strategies for minorities to succeed, regardless of the current environment.

Chapter 11, "How Can I Progress?"

In this chapter, we talk about how to move forward in your career, including whether to become a technical specialist or generalist and, generally, how to move around the field.

Chapter 12, "Should I Manage People?"

Here, we will examine what it takes to be a people manager in security and whether management is a good fit for you.

Chapter 13, "How Can I Deal With Imposter Syndrome?"

Many security people suffer from imposter syndrome. We unpack what that means and how to deal with it.

Chapter 14, "How Can I Know If It's Time To Move On?"

In this chapter, we consider the factors to consider before you move to your next position and why you might want to stay where you are.

The questions in these chapters were chosen to help you navigate your working life as a security professional with intention and grace. When you were searching for your first security job, I asked you to consider *why* you wanted it: why this job, why this company, and why in this place? As you progress through your career, the "why" question is still the most important, and now you have more information to consider as you answer it. Keep your answers handy, adjust them when needed, and use these questions to help enjoy your security career.

CHAPTER

8

How Do I Keep Up?

Summary

- **Know yourself:** Plan for what you want to learn and follow it. Start with your immediate job and work outward from there.
- **Network:** Ask your network for recommendations about learning resources. Find social media, curated security news, and online learning sources.
- **Stay curious:** Go deep on a few chosen topics. Read, watch, and listen to a wide variety of resources.
- **Communicate well and often:** Share what you've learned with colleagues and your network.

Even before you get a job in security, it becomes glaringly obvious that a lot of change is happening, and there are lots of things to learn.

There is change in technology. There are new technology products emerging. There are new ways of using old technology. There are new security tools to address the new technology. This change is happening exponentially. New technology is being introduced and adopted faster each year. Staying ahead of what the technology is and what it means for security practitioners is challenging. Currently, we are looking at artificial intelligence and 5G, just to name a couple of things, and we are trying to work out what threats they create for an organization, how each security function will need to adjust to deal with those threats, and whether those threats are big enough to bump another security goal off the list of priorities.

Then there are changes in the way people use technology. Changes in where, how, and when people work mean the security profile of an organization changes, too. The shift to working from home in response to the pandemic meant technology and security teams had to scramble to ensure working remotely was enabled securely. The adoption of mobile devices and cloud applications made the traditional network "castle and moat" approach to security (do an internet search for "zero-trust networking" for more on this) much less relevant. The desire to use less paper and be less tethered to a physical location changed the way we monitor and respond to incidents.

Closer to home, new leadership can result in new organizational priorities. When this happens, the security leader and the team need to refocus their security priorities, too. Maybe the organization wants to work in a new geographic region. Perhaps there are mergers and acquisitions, and now the security team needs to learn a new business with new technologies and new regulations. Perhaps the new leader wants to shrink the organization, and the threat of a disgruntled insider threat becomes much more urgent. Organizational change can be hard to predict and even harder to respond to.

Regulations are created and keep getting more intrusive and prescriptive. The regulation might come from a federal government, an industry regulator, a data regulator, or even through contracts. With new regulation comes new security requirements, which require new learning and new ways of performing security duties. Worse, the regulations often overlap or contradict one another. Knowing which regulations apply to a security person's role, team, or company is hard to do. Entire subindustries of security law and compliance have sprung up to help companies manage these regulations. There are many levels of compliance that need to be considered. Keeping up with regulations isn't easy and the need to do so won't be going anywhere anytime soon.

If you are working in security, you will be expected to stay current with all these trends. Companies don't give their security staff much time to do this, so your responsibility will be carving out time and space to keep learning. There are two pieces to this: how to organize your time to make room for learning and how to find the best resources to make learning as efficient as possible.

Fitting It Into Your Schedule

Before you try to keep up with everything, you need to decide what your focus will be. There is too much going on for you to keep up with all the changing security landscape. My recommendation is to take the onion approach. That is, start from where you are and work outward from there.

- Your primary goal is to know what you need to know to be successful in your current job. For example, if you are working in security training and awareness functions, find time to learn all you can about how to do that job. Learn about the tools you use daily, the procedures you need to follow, and the reporting you need to produce. Learn what your other teammates do and how they do it. Understand how your role and theirs fit together. Obtain the knowledge and skills to be successful in that role — however your manager and company define success.

- Once you have the "how to do my immediate job" learning planned out, you should broaden your horizon to other industry-related items. For example, if you are working as an incident responder, start learning about current industry issues in incident response, such as by reading threat intelligence feeds, creating and managing playbooks, or industry-standard incident response tools. You should get to know the leading thinkers in this space, as well as the vendors who offer security tools/products in incident response. You should learn about vendor strengths and weaknesses.
- Think about adjacent spaces, and plan to learn at least enough about those areas to be conversant. For example, if you do third-party risk assessments, learn about penetration testing, also known as *ethical hacking*. Understand passive and active testing. Know how those roles align with your own.
- Once you know your role and you are conversant about industry issues related to it, it is time to think about your next role. What kind of job do you want after this one? What do you need to learn to be ready for it? The next role might be a step up the ladder from where you are now, so learning more about your current function would be great. You might want to move into a different security role, so include learning about the new function in your learning plan. If you

don't know what comes next, pick something that looks interesting and learn about that. There is no downside to learning more!

- Regardless of your role, industry, or seniority, you should always be making time to learn about current events. Learning what's hot in the industry will help you excel at your current role, and it will help you see what your future roles might look like. Keeping up with current incidents, emerging security trends, and news appearing in nonsecurity media outlets will help you with your current role and help when you look for your next one.
- Know your history. While some security-related topics might seem new and unique, we are seeing a lot of repeat behavior, too. Knowing the past will help you plan better for the future.

Within these learning categories, you can pick topics and spend two weeks or a month learning as much as you can. Once you've learned what you planned to learn, move on to the next thing.

Once you have the list of things you want to pay attention to, you must then find a way to fit learning time into your schedule. Most companies are happy to pay for some level of formal training in which you take classes or attend a yearly conference. Increasingly, companies are contracting with online learning resources that offer on-demand learning. While many companies don't offer any kind of training, you should definitely take advantage of any training your company makes available to you. Make sure it aligns with your focus areas as much as you can, though relying on once-a-year training isn't going to be enough to stay up-to-date on security issues and concerns.

Ad Hoc and Planned Learning

To make this all work, you will need a combination of ad hoc and planned learning. Ad hoc learning is when you randomly pick up pieces of information from something as simple as listening to a security podcast on your way to work, while you're walking the dog, or while you're eating breakfast. It can mean following targeted security people on social media (more on this below) and scrolling through your feeds to see what looks interesting.

> Ad hoc learning doesn't have to take dedicated focus and deep thought.

Ad hoc learning is a passive way of absorbing high-level information on a range of topics. This is great for learning about current events or industry trends.

Planned learning requires dedicated headspace time to learn and absorb. It's certainly reasonable to carve out time on your work calendar to learn more about how to do your immediate job. If your role allows it, find work calendar time available to block out so you can do reading about your immediate industry or even your next role. Some people like to schedule an hour or so each week and dedicate that hour to reading articles, books, or social media feeds specifically related to those topics. Some use the time to actively practice skills in their home lab or work sandbox.

The longer you're in the industry, the more you will realize that the things you need to learn cannot be easily contained in a 40-hour workweek. Some people do it, but more of us find time to do learning outside working hours. If you can't do your learning during your standard workweek, I would recommend making a structured learning plan. Perhaps you get up early and read for an hour, or perhaps you can read or watch online content for an hour before bed. Perhaps you spend some dedicated time on the weekend working in your lab. You might decide to attend security conferences or watch virtual events during personal time off work.

Take a Mini-Sabbatical

Here's a final suggestion: once a quarter, if you can, take a full day off to focus on your learning and evaluate your career plan. You'll likely need it to play catch-up for the things you wanted to learn about but didn't have the time. Many companies will be okay letting you take that day on company time. If not, consider taking it as a personal day. The break from the rest of your work life will be a mini-vacation, and you will be able to dedicate your brain to an uninterrupted day of learning. It is well worth the investment.

I'm not recommending you spend your entire waking life thinking about security — that's not healthy. Instead, I am suggesting you plan what you want to learn and structure your time for when you want to learn it. This way, you can take comfort in knowing that you are making time to keep up with the industry and be prepared for your next career step.

Where Do I Find the Information?

Finding and curating information about security is a challenge for even the most seasoned security professionals. There is so much information out there. Knowing where to find quality information is hard when you're just learning the space. As you build your library of resources, it will become easier. Consider the following points:

- **Talk to your team:** Networking within your own company is good for the job you do now and the roles you want in the future. While you are talking to your team, ask them what resources they use. Who do they follow on social media? What social media platforms are they on? What security websites/magazines/books would they recommend you consume? Who is a good and knowledgeable resource in the company? Do they have any books about your preferred subject that they could recommend (or even lend you)?

- **Self-study:** Pick some online learning classes and take them. Decide if you find them useful (if so, take more classes from the same company). Of course, if you don't find a particular class useful, you should be wary of taking additional classes offered by the same company. These classes will often recommend other resources, so use them. Find books on the topic you're interested in and find time to read or listen to them. (Audiobooks are great if you don't have time to sit still.) Most resources will give you suggestions for other resources. Follow the learning trail it creates.
- **Conferences and professional boot camps:** These are learning opportunities in and of themselves — great. You are also in a room with a bunch of other people with whom you can network and share thoughts. While you're in class or standing in the lunch line, ask people what resources they use to learn more about your topic of interest.
- **Analyst resources:** For a fee, there are security analysis companies that will provide researched articles about security trends. Access to these usually requires a corporate subscription. If you are fortunate enough to work in a company with a subscription to companies like Gartner, Forrester, or others, take advantage of their content. Sometimes, content is published for free, so keep your eye out for those.

- **Security publications:** There are several industry news outlets with websites and email subscription offerings. These typically give a good balance of current events and broader trends. It is almost impossible to read all of them all the time, so pick a couple and spend some time with them during your structured learning time.
- **Social and streaming media:** In terms of real-time current affairs, nothing beats social media to have instant access to events. There are lots of sources to choose from — Twitter, LinkedIn, RSS feeds, and influencers' blogs and postings. I check in with these feeds a couple of times a day to keep up with daily events. Podcasts are particularly useful for learning about emerging concepts, issues of the day, and the backstory behind current news events. Podcasts will take up an hour or so of your time, so they're great for commuting time, work breaks, or after hours. Connect with people who are recommended by others, and don't be afraid to disconnect if they're not useful to you.

The amount of information out there can be overwhelming. Some security folks have curated their information into consolidated Twitter or Slack feeds so that they can be more efficient in their consumption. Sometimes, you can get the information you need, when you need it, simply by managing your time better.

What's Next?

- Take time to decide how you want to focus your learning in the next month.
- Spend some time putting blocks on your work calendar for learning — at least an hour each week if you can.

- If necessary, schedule time on your personal calendar to listen to podcasts, read a book, or watch a video.
- Talk to your team and ask them where they get their information. Set up your own social media or email subscriptions to start receiving that information, too.

CHAPTER

9

How Can I Manage Security Stress?

Summary

- **Take care of yourself first:** Stress can be positive, but negative stress impacts your personal and professional life. Do what you can to implement habits that reduce the impact of stress.
- **Security stress is unique:** It might be caused by others not understanding security, by security people prioritizing security above business objectives, or by leaders who think of security as an expense instead of as a strategic enabler.

- **Minimize stress:** Teach others about the benefits of security, align security with business outcomes, and get some sleep!
- **Network:** Get ideas on how to minimize security stress. Mingle with people who understand what you're dealing with.
- **Stay curious:** Teach your partners why security is important to you, and learn how to incorporate security into their roles in a meaningful way.

Let me begin by recognizing that stress is not inherently bad. Stress can be positive, too. Good stress can help us perform better, reach higher, and move faster. It can energize us and motivate us to do more. This chapter is not about that kind of stress. In this chapter, we will discuss negative stress — the kind that raises your cortisol levels, makes you anxious, and generally wears you down.

In the beginning of a career, stress is often caused by workload. Perhaps you have too much work to do and you aren't sure how to prioritize yourself. Perhaps you have not yet learned how to negotiate your workload with your manager. Sometimes the stress is because you have not yet learned the skills to make doing the assigned work as easy as possible, and the skills gap causes you stress. You are still learning the tools of the trade and how to get things done in your organization. The combination is sometimes overwhelming. In the beginning, it's easy to think that the stress you face is because of you — and your lack of experience or skills — and often, this is the case. Only time and perseverance can address this problem. The good news is that it's a fixable issue and one that other people around you expect you to face, so they are likely to help you manage it. There are also lots of resources available to help you manage the stress of learning new things.

Once you have been working for a while and you are proficient in your current job, the things that cause stress will change. Now, the things that cause stress will not be caused by your inexperience; instead, stress will occur as you interact with more people, and you begin to see how well your organization manages stress-causing events and processes.

> Given a few years of experience, the source of your stress changes from internal to external, and how to address the stress changes with it.

Now, you have more difficult decisions to make. You can't just learn your way out of a problem (or leave!). You will need to be intentional, patient, and strategic.

If you work anywhere in any profession for long enough, you'll experience stress. Stress comes in many flavors, and you'll experience most of them. Stress doesn't just impact your work. It impacts your personal life, your family, and your health. Just do an internet search on *managing work stress*, and you will find thousands of articles. It's a chronic problem!

The Stress of Working in Security

Security work has its own form of stress-inducing work, but why is it uniquely stressful?

- Security professionals are evangelists. They believe in the value of security as an integral part of the success of any organization, and they see their role and the functions they provide as being vital to achieving the organizational mission.

This tendency to prioritize security over other mission objectives causes misunderstandings and conflicts with nonsecurity people. This leads to security people calling their customers "stupid" and generally means that getting anything done takes longer than expected. Security people understand that having security controls in place allows a company to move faster. Nonsecurity people understand security controls to be speed bumps in their road to success. As a result, it often takes longer than expected to get things done. Security people must spend time dealing with the customer's psychology before they can even begin to talk about security requirements or solutions. Nonsecurity people feel the tension between their own work goals and the often-conflicting security needs. This disconnect frustrates everyone.

- Nonsecurity people don't understand what security is or what it does. It seems to be some vaguely technical, shadowy activity that is called upon when bad things happen. This results in security personnel being left out of strategic or general business planning sessions and are called in only at the last minute to fix things that would've been cheaper and easier to fix if security had been consulted earlier in the process. This means security teams are spending more time firefighting than delivering planned security improvements. And it means the nonsecurity people must stop what they're doing and pay attention to security when they'd much rather be doing what they are paid to do.
- Security costs money, and it's often difficult to trace that money directly to the organization's revenue, which leads to a lack of executive support. Some leaders have seen firsthand the impact of a data breach and the negative impact on the company when things go wrong. They think of security

like insurance — a necessary evil that needs to be funded, rather than a strategic enabler of business value. They don't want to spend money on security because they don't see the point in spending money to protect something that might not need protecting. This is typical risk-taking psychology. People defer difficult decisions until they are forced to face them, which means security teams are chronically underfunded. It is like watching a car accident occur in slow motion for security people. They can see the impact that will occur, but they are powerless to prevent it. It means that when something bad inevitably happens, the security team might be able to say, "I told you so," but then they have to jump in to fix the problem with limited resources. No matter how satisfying it might be to say "I told you so," saying it doesn't make anyone feel better.

- Because security isn't built into a tool or service from the start, security controls are bolted on after the fact (if at all). These security controls have a negative impact on customer experience (more clicks, more passwords, and more cost), and they are often jettisoned at the first sign of customer concern. Typically, a rush to market means less security, which results in the security team having to convince partners and customers that the inconvenience is worth the risk. Because customers and partners don't believe the risk is imminent or impactful, this is a hard case to make.
- When security is done well, nothing happens. When security is done well, something bad might happen anyway. This dichotomy calls into question the value of the existing security team. No one likes being second-guessed, but security teams are particularly exposed to being second-guessed in ways that other professions are not.

- In the security profession, we look for and find the bad things that are happening. We look for malware, ransomware, and indicators of compromise. We are made aware of insiders doing dubious or illegal things. We receive advisories about nation-state attacks. We spend our time thinking about what could go wrong and how bad the impact would be if it did. And we keep this to ourselves. In the name of security and in the name of protecting people from unnecessary worry, we don't share this stuff outside the security team. And when others do hear about the things we know, they ask, "how can you sleep at night?"
- Security people have a difficult time turning off and getting away from work. Adversaries are working 24/7, so we tend to be thinking about security stuff even when we are not at work. It's too easy to never shut down and take the mental and physical breaks we need.

So, there you are, a skilled security professional, using your skills and experience to help the organization secure its information and systems, and the organization is pushing back — security is too slow, too expensive, and too hard to understand. The organization pushes back on you until something bad happens, which is when your professional skill might be questioned. In other words, you are damned if you do, damned if you don't.

This kind of stress makes itself known as soon as you're put in a situation where you have to try to influence someone who doesn't want to spend the money, make the change, or understand the risk. In other words, almost every security person at every level faces this chasm of disconnection sooner or later.

In addition to all the usual stresses — too many priorities, work-life balance, obnoxious co-workers, and unskilled management — a security person must also layer on security stress. Are you sure you want to work in this profession?

Managing Security Stress

If you're going to work in security, you will need to learn to manage this stress. You must have much higher emotional intelligence than other people. Consider reading Daniel Goleman's book, *Emotional Intelligence*, to help you hone your EI skills. You're going to have to spend time working with others and helping them understand where you are coming from and why. You're also going to have to spend time working to change their outlook on you and the security agenda. You will need to take care of yourself with diet, exercise, sleep, and other strategies, *and* you will need to address the security elephant in the room. And you will need to let go when there are people who won't understand security, no matter how hard you try. This isn't just for security leaders. Everyone working in security needs to manage security stress. The following sections contain some suggestions.

Teach Them

Security stress is often caused by nonsecurity people not knowing what you do. This is a relatively easy problem to fix. Find your customers and your closest IT partners and spend time with them. Learn about what they do, and tell them how security supports their work. Let them know how the security team enables their best work, stops their systems from being unavailable at the worst possible time, and ensures they don't get fined by regulators (or go to jail). Share with them how you do your job and what it takes to be the security professional that you are. If they can better understand your role and you can better understand theirs, it is more likely that they'll support you when needed. This reduces stress better than anything else!

Sometimes it's hard to remember that most people around you want to be a good partner — they just don't know how.

Assume positive intent on their part. These aren't the noisy people who make you grind your teeth and self-medicate to manage stress. These are the silent people who just do what they do without giving security a lot of thought. Don't assume that they magically know how your job is done. They're too busy trying to do their own jobs. Instead, take the initiative to reach out and help them understand your role. This requires personal relationships, so be strategic about who you approach. You will need to engage in one-on-discussions, possibly over coffee or lunch. This person might be your primary partner, but they might also be someone who is a "social connector," who will spread the word to others about what you do. Time is precious — use it wisely.

Find Common Causes

"I'm going to go to work today and make my product/service/company the most secure ever!" said no one ever. If you're a security person, don't talk to other people about the security objective. They just won't care enough for the conversation to matter. Instead, find out what matters to them — a product launch, cost management, new markets, a server build, and so on — and overlap the security work to that objective.

Sometimes, people will leave you out of important discussions, only do the minimum necessary to satisfy security requirements, and make decisions that result in more work for you or your team. When you encounter someone like this who is particularly difficult to work with, try focusing specifically on that person. Find time to meet with them and ask about them and their nonsecurity needs. Understand their "why." Understand what and who is motivating them — their goals and objectives — and how they do their work.

Once you know where they are coming from, tailor any messaging to that "why." If they care about availability of services (no outages!), then talk about how security supports system availability. If they care about cost, talk about how engaging security early will keep costs low. If they care about time to market, let them know that engaging security early will prevent rework and lost time.

Often, particularly with IT partners, security is overlooked in the name of "customer experience." This is a false dichotomy. The way to handle this stress is to find stories that talk about the positive customer experience that happened *because* of security requirements. For example, one company implemented a security framework that required network engineers to inventory their IP addresses. At first, the network group grumbled. Then they did it, and they found stale IP addresses that could be freed up and reused, saving them money and time. Another company implemented multifactor authentication. The customer service teams were concerned that the added login step would be a negative customer experience. When customers learned they could use the same interface for their personal security (banking and the like), they saw it as a positive action to help them. Find examples like these and use them in your conversations with IT partners and others.

Advise Them, and Then Let Them Decide

A challenge for most security professionals is that we really, really believe that our perspective is correct and that disregarding our suggestions will lead to bad things. While this is probably true, this perspective doesn't recognize that other people in an organization must weigh many factors when making their choices.

Security is just one factor among many. Ultimately, the decision to implement a security control or fund a security initiative is a business decision to be made by them, not by the security team.

Make sure that the decision-making structure in your organization enables the right people to be the decision-makers. For example, if a decision is made to not patch a vulnerability on a server, who makes that decision? Is it the server administrator? The service owner who uses the server? The business VP who uses the service? If there is an exception process, who approves that exception? Depending on where you are in the organization, you might not have the authority to fix a bad governance structure if it's broken. Do what you can, and then raise your concerns through appropriate management channels.

If you suggest a course of action and they reject your advice, or if they file an exception to an otherwise agreed upon process and the right person approves it, that's okay. Don't take it personally, and don't let the rejected advice make you think that all future advice will be disregarded. (If you actually *are* finding your advice being always ignored, that's another story. See Chapter 14, "How Can I Know if It's Time to Move On?") Being able to separate your personal feelings from a business decision will help you recognize that your value isn't because you are obeyed all the time. Your value is to provide solid information and advice to others who can choose to take it — or not. Regardless of their choice, your job is done well.

Lead with Principles

Early in my security career, I tried to justify the cost and design of security using metrics and benchmarks. It was logically the thing to do — any MBA graduate would agree. The problem is that for most organizations, security isn't a revenue stream (unless you work for a security product company). It looks like a cost center, and if the perceived business value of security is that nothing bad happens, it's really hard to prove the return on investment of security when it is invisible.

There's nothing inherently wrong with benchmarks or metrics per se. There's definitely a lot of industry confusion about which metrics are meaningful and which ones provide the right context for your story. Even if you find the perfect metric to use, it can't be the focus of the discussion. Instead, you need to share your principles — the *why* of security — before trying to convince other people to invest time, money, or people in security. (Simon Sinek's book *Start with Why* is a good resource to help you frame your own "why".) So, if your *why* is availability, tell stories about how security ensures technology systems are available when and where you need them. If your *why* is data protection and privacy, tell stories about how your program ensures people can trust what the company is doing.

Nonsecurity people don't need to know how security works; they just have to agree that the reason security exists — that your role exists — is important to them.

Get Some Sleep

There is always something scary happening in security. Keeping up with all the breaches, nation-state attacks, and insider threats is enough to keep you up 24 hours a day. But you need to be able to step away from this and recharge. Be clear with yourself about what you can do and what you can't, and make sure you are doing the things you can. Let the rest go. If you've done what you are meant to do, then you can go to sleep at night regardless of the rest of the noise that continues to swirl. If you've shared your security concerns with your company and the company has chosen to accept the risk anyway, then you've done your job. Get some rest.

These strategies are just as relevant for a junior security analyst as they are for a senior security executive. Creating partners who understand your *why* as much as you understand theirs helps with managing your security stress. And who doesn't need that?

What's Next?

- Build relationships with people who can help you manage the factors that lead to security stress.
- Get the basics under control: sleep, exercise, diet, and so on. Take care of yourself first.
- Take stock of your work situation. Can you identify the source of your stress? A skills gap? A difficult co-worker? The work culture? All the above?
- Plan to intentionally improve/remove the stress. Try it out for the next couple of months.
- Define where your job stops and starts and what you can personally own. Make sure you're not taking responsibility for security stuff outside your role.
- Talk to your network. Have they experienced this? If so, how did they handle it?

CHAPTER 10

How Can I Succeed as a Minority?

Summary

- **Know yourself:** Consider how vocal and visible you want to be in promoting issues of equity and inclusion.
- **Network:** Join internal and external networking groups that identify with your status and use them for support and guidance
- **Be intentional:** If you find yourself flexing your personality to stay in a role, team, or company, consider what you will do to improve the situation — up to and including leaving.

The security profession has a problem. It is both an image problem and a systemic functional problem. The workforce is way too homogeneous. It is made up primarily of men, and in most countries, it is made up of cisgender men who are white and straight, which to a degree is far out of step with the proportions of the general population. Security workers who are not cis-male, white, and straight must take additional actions to ensure that they are hired, trained, included, promoted, and valued because of their work, not because of or despite their non-majority attributes.

The impact of this imbalance is significant. When young people don't see themselves as a potential member of a technology tribe in middle school, they opt out of taking classes that would lead them to a traditional security career route. When working women hear stories of male-dominated security jobs, they choose a different career option. When minority people working in security don't see themselves reflected in the leadership team, they leave the industry to go where they can see themselves. This makes our hiring pipeline too small and too leaky. It isn't deep or wide enough, so we are experiencing labor shortages. This puts pressure on people already in the industry to work longer hours and do more with less. It puts pressure on hiring companies, and there is a war for talent, which costs money. It means that there is less diversity of thought within security teams — and we need diverse and creative thinking to address the security issues of the day. Finally, it creates stress for minority employees who want to know that their contributions are valued and appreciated and who must be concerned about workplace environments.

Other kinds of "minority" status also affect a person's ability to succeed. Age, marital status, disability status, parent status, location, and educational background can also play a role in determining how easily someone fits with the existing culture.

In security, there is the technical versus nontechnical dichotomy to deal with as well. These can impact white straight men, too. Over the course of our careers, few of us will be immune to some form of bias that will make it harder to succeed.

What does this mean for minorities working in security? This looks different for everyone, but here are some things it can mean:

- Being the only minority status person on a security team, where your performance is judged on your personal performance *and* through others' perceptions of your gender, race, or other minority affiliation.
- Being asked to represent your minority group within or outside the organization, adding work to an already full load.
- Receiving less-direct and useful performance feedback during coaching or performance reviews (if you are female).
- Trying to balance fitting into the majority work culture, while remaining authentic to your own style, values, and traditions that might not align with the majority.
- Being asked to prove readiness for a higher role before promotion, if you are a minority worker, rather than being given the role based on anticipated capability, if you are in the majority.
- Evaluating new companies, teams, and roles based on your understanding of their support of minority issues, which typically look good on paper but reveal themselves after you've already taken the role.
- Earning a job or a promotion and having others (and sometimes yourself) question whether you received it because you were the "best candidate" or because you are the "minority candidate."

It sounds overwhelming. The good news is that many in the industry are aware of the problem and are working to fix it. The onus is on those in the majority to make changes to support inclusion and equity for minority workers, and many are already doing this work. It will take a long time because the root of the problem lies outside the security industry and in the societal cultures in which we live. Culture change is hard. But there are steps that the security industry, companies, and managers can take to improve the situation. (For more, see Chapter 19, "How Do I Encourage Diversity and Inclusion?") In the meantime, minority security professionals have resources to help them succeed in the current environment.

My Story

As a woman in security, I've been in the minority status for most of my career. I was often the only woman on the team, the only female manager, and the only female person in the meeting.

Once, I was attending a security conference with some of my team. The four people I was with all happened to be men. We walked into the room, and a security salesman walked over to us and introduced himself. He shook everyone's hand except mine and then asked, "where is your CISO?" My team pointed at me. He turned red in the face, and it got awkward quickly.

This kind of incident didn't happen often, nor was it an unexpected experience working in this industry. Sometimes, it was caused by inherent bias. Sometimes, it was caused by ignorance. Sometimes, it was blatant misogyny. This has happened in every company I've worked and in every role

I've held. Sometimes, the incidents were minor, like this one. Sometimes, they were bigger. As a woman in security, I am not alone in my experience.

I owe my career to male allies who have guided and supported me. It was, after all, a man who first asked me to work in technology and who hired me for my first management role. It was a man who hired me into my first security position. I'm married to a man who supports my work every day (and night). I've worked with fabulous male colleagues who go out of their way to attract, welcome, and encourage minority security professionals. Those same men continue to learn about the challenges of being a minority and how they can encourage diversity and inclusivity. I am a leader in security because of the support, mentorship, and sponsorship of men — and I am grateful for their advocacy. I've also been evaluated as "pushy" when being assertive, mistaken for the administrative assistant, inappropriately approached by a colleague, and dealt with other microaggressions too numerous to name.

Most men cannot fully appreciate what a woman's experience in technology is, any more than I can fully appreciate the experience of people with backgrounds different from my own. I speak out to let men know that it's not just the one woman on their team or me. I want other minority professionals to know they are not alone in their experiences. I want to expose biased behavior so we can collectively change it.

Being in more of a senior position gives me the power (and typically, it is about power) to speak on these issues with less risk. I have an obligation to use my position to influence the changes needed to allow security to diversify its membership.

Making Security Work for You

You cannot exist professionally without being part of a larger ecosystem of colleagues, partners, and potential adversaries. You must find a way to be part of the community and be true to your own experiences and values. Otherwise, you will eventually burn out and leave the industry. How can that be done? There is no right way (of course!), but here are some thoughts.

Find Your Community

If you don't work in a company with employee networking groups, or even if you do, you might find it useful to join external organizations that promote and support diversity and inclusion. Women in Cybersecurity (WiCyS), the International Consortium of Minority Cyber Professionals (ICMCP), and other groups provide resources to employers and employees to provide a lifeline where needed.

Why join groups like this?

- People in these groups often have similar experiences as yourself. They can be a sympathetic ear if you experience challenges. They can offer solutions you can use to try to address problems you are facing. When things are difficult at work, it can be hard to determine if it is caused by your own weaknesses or by bias and/or lack of inclusivity and equity in the team. Having a group of people outside your immediate workplace can give you some perspective to help you navigate this sensitive question.
- These groups are a great network to help you find opportunities with future employers or ways to expand your influence. They can help you speak at conferences or on

panels; they can recommend employers to consider (or not) for future positions. Most importantly, they can lift you up when you need it.

Be an Advocate

I don't like when the [insert minority status here] person is called to do the work of getting the rest of the organization to think and act more inclusively. I also know, however, that unless minorities engage with the groups in power to move them to change their behavior, it won't happen. Part of the challenge of being a minority is balancing these ideas. Worse, in some particularly toxic places, being a person who speaks for the minority can be seen as a career-limiting move. You are going to have to know your environment and act accordingly.

We can speak for our own needs in a way that isn't confrontational (asking others to change can be perceived as confrontational), is professional, and allows us to express our values without alienating other groups. For example, we can do the following:

- Lead diversity initiatives on a team, a suborganization, or the whole company. Of course, larger organizations might already have a chief diversity officer or something similar. Get to know what they're doing and how you can engage. If they or your team doesn't seem to have a focus on diversity issues, suggest to your manager that you would be willing to take this on.
- Represent ourselves by speaking publicly at our companies or in the security community. The topic doesn't have to be about diversity and inclusion. In fact, one of the best ways to dispel negative stereotypes about minorities is to talk about technical/core professional issues. Being visible is, in and of itself, an act of advocacy.

If getting up in front of people isn't your thing, being a one-on-one advocate is a great way to go.

- Offering advice to others who ask for it can be a great way to help others on their journeys. Be a mentor to other minorities, particularly on the security team as well as in adjacent functions. (Recruiting more minorities to security is a good thing!)
- Helping ally partners is hugely impactful. If you know someone in the majority who is trying to be an ally, reach out and offer your support. Be available to help them as they ask for it.

Talking about the things that are important to you is an important step toward having power. Be careful, though. This kind of work is *not* a hobby — it is work, and you should make sure you are given space to do it as part of your paid job. Extra time, extra credit, and extra pay are all good things to negotiate before taking on additional work.

Find Your Workplace Allies

In every place I have worked, I have faced a negative situation because I was female in a male-dominated culture. And in those same places, I've found male sponsors, mentors, partners, and friends who have helped me navigate those challenges and succeed anyway. While it would be preferable to work in a culture that treated everyone equitably and inclusively, we work with people who bring their own personalities, biases, and cultures to work with them.

Finding workplace allies starts with the people you work with all the time. They don't have to be on your immediate team; they simply need to be someone who knows who you are and what you do. Build relationships with the people you find trustworthy. Don't stop with one person. Find a team of people — your own "board of directors" — who can act as your sounding board and can give you clear-eyed advice and feedback on situations that arise. If they're in your minority group, great. But sometimes you won't have that option, so don't limit yourself to only that group.

If you work for a larger organization, there might be employee networking groups that can speak to your concerns. Women in Technology groups, LGBTQ organizations, and People of Color in Technology are just some of the groups you can join. While internal networking groups are not likely to be specific to security, they are a community of people who have likely encountered some of the same challenges.

Find your personal support crew who can lift you up when you need it. I promise, they exist.

Consider the Alternative

I once left a particularly stressful role that was made more stressful by the way women leaders were perceived in the masculine culture of the organization. It was a difficult decision to leave, but it was the right move to make in hindsight. Later, a colleague remarked, "You had to flex your personality to work there." And he was right. Until I left, I didn't realize the amount of physical and mental stress I was carrying to work in an environment where I had to modify my actions to fit in with the majority culture.

These days, you cannot segregate your work life from your personal life. So, if you feel that you must hide your true self to work at that place or that you are constantly facing unreasonable obstacles, consider other options. It might not be immediately possible. Finding a good role worthy of making an effort to leave can take time. But empower yourself to find the right role.

We will continue to make positive progress toward a workplace that is diverse, inclusive, and equitable. Until then, we need to hold true to ourselves and make sure the places we work support our personal selves and the people around us. Stay strong!

What's Next?

- Find your support network. If your current network doesn't include those with whom you can comfortably discuss these issues, consider adding to your network. Look for people inside and outside your organization who can be your allies.
- Consider your role in managing diversity, inclusion, and equity issues at your company. Do you want to be a vocal advocate or a quiet one?
- Evaluate your current work environment, particularly your manager. Do you feel supported? Are you included? Are you treated equitably? If not, what are you willing to do about it? Can you influence change? Is it time to consider leaving or affecting change from within?

CHAPTER

11

How Can I Progress?

Summary

- **Keep learning:** Think of your career like an apprenticeship: apprentice, journeyperson, and expert. Know which stage you are in.
- **Be an opportunist:** Stay current with security trends, network with others, and formalize your learning with certifications or degrees.
- **Be intentional, but stay flexible:** If you know what you want to do next, research what is needed, and make sure your work experience and learning give you those things. Find people who are in the next role you want and ask them for advice.

- **Stay curious:** Keep learning about people and things that will take you to the next step in your career — skills, experiences, and contacts.
- **Communicate well and often:** Promote your work, particularly to your network, manager, and sponsor.

When we are children in school, we inevitably meet the kid who knows exactly what they want to be when they grow up. They are unwavering in their pursuit of whatever that is. They take all the right classes, do all the right summer camps, get relevant internships, and generally move intentionally through their career. Then there are the rest of us who have no clear idea of what we want to do for a job, how to move from one phase to another, or how to know that we're on the right path — if there even is a path.

When it comes to chasing a successful security career, most people are still in one of these camps. Some people know early that they want to be an ethical hacker. Some know that running a compliance team is exactly their role in life. Some know that their goal is to be a CISO. Then there are the rest of us who vaguely want to "work in security." Once there, we aren't sure where we want to go next. We might like to be a security engineer focusing on vulnerability management, or we might want to lead the security awareness and training program — either looks good. We might see a manager we really want to work for — so we are less picky about exactly what role we take. This holds true even for senior-level security leaders. Some have a career plan that they are faithfully executing. Others still don't know what they want to be when they grow up.

By the time someone has been in role for a couple of years, they start to ask themselves how they can progress, and there is, of course, no easy answer. But there are some things to consider.

The Security Journey

Regardless of which path you are on, think about your career in phases like a traditional apprenticeship.

- In the beginning (the first three to five years), you are an apprentice — learning mostly on the job the basic skills you need to be a security professional. Even with a degree, the first few years are spent working out what it means to be in security. Often, you're doing operational work and less project work. You're usually working beside/under someone who is responsible for teaching you the skills you need.
- After the first five years or so, you become a journeyperson. Working with more independence, you start to focus on certain kinds of security work and honing your skills by taking on different projects. You might start teaching more junior people, even if they don't report to you. You get out in the security community more often, learning from others and not just your own company. But you're not yet ready to be called an "expert."
- Expertise takes time. And even in an industry as fast-paced as technology/security, becoming an expert doesn't happen overnight. Typically, this happens somewhere between 10 to 20 years of working in the industry. Oh, you can get the title of Director, VP, or even CISO faster than 10 years, but

the experience you need to truly be regarded as an "expert" (a loaded term if there ever was one) can't happen overnight. As an expert, you are not just a functional expert; you are a thought leader for your company (if it's big enough) or your slice of the industry. You teach others and are sought out by others as a source of information.

Which phase of your career are you in, and how do you progress through to the next one?

The Opportunist

For many of us, we are asked where we want to be in 2, 5, 10, or 20 years, and we often answer, "I have no idea." If this is you, the question then is this: are you prepared for when the next opportunity presents itself? Well, how do you prepare for something if you don't know what it is?

If you're currently in a smaller company, it's likely that you are already a generalist — most small firms can't afford people who specialize too much. You might do a lot of different things — vulnerability management, configuration management, security testing, and incident response. This is great, but perhaps being "an inch deep and a mile wide" won't give you enough functional experience to jump up to the next level. Alternatively, if you are working in a large company, you are likely specializing in only one or two functions. You can talk deeply about one function but have zero experience in other areas. If you want to stay in those functions, great, but it will limit your ability to take roles in other areas. So big or small, generalist or specialist, how can you be prepared for the next opportunity?

Stay Current with Security Issues and Trends

There are a million resources available to help you keep current on security issues, and if you're a generalist, these resources can help you dig deeper into a topic you already know, including magazines, blogs, podcasts, and conferences. Find time each week to dip into any one of these resources and simply look around. Listen to podcasts while you are walking the dog or driving places. Subscribe to magazines and curated digital sources that send you daily digests and read them in the morning before you start work. At conferences, attend topics outside your normal areas just to hear what people are talking about.

You might find something particularly interesting; feel free to chase that topic down the rabbit hole. Read the references from articles, Google the topic, or email the author of a book or article with more questions. Use social media to "poll" your community about their thoughts on the topic — they will always teach you something new!

> You might find something that looks awful; well, now you know not to pursue it any further. Understanding what you don't like is just as important as understanding what you do. It helps you narrow your thinking and choices about the next role you might consider.

Don't just learn about stuff you already know. Instead, look for things you don't know. If the amount of unknown stuff is intimidating, start with things adjacent to your current field. For example, if you're working in application security, look more into containers, API security, or pentesting. If you are working in incident response, consider looking into threat intelligence or encryption solutions more deeply. Check out security mindmaps to see what other functions are considered part of "security," and chase one of those paths.

Network

Getting to know security people is the best way to be available for opportunities. They can let you know what they're working on, what's coming in the future, and which skills they value.

Know the people in your company who can help you move to a different or bigger role. This starts with your immediate manager — they need to know when you're ready for something new or are thinking about trying something new. If they're not open to helping you into a new position, ask them why. Maybe they think you're not ready — important information to have, even if you disagree. A manager should always be your advocate. If you learn that they want to keep you in your current role when you're ready to move, consider finding a new manager!

Consider intentionally networking with people in your company who are not part of your immediate team. Find out what they do, and let them know what you do in return. Choose people who can assist you in your career development at the company, and let them know you are working toward your next role. If your company is large enough, find influential security leaders. If your company is small, find primary partners/customers who know your work. These people can identify potential projects or job opportunities early and can advocate for you. They will open doors of opportunity for you.

Most importantly, network with people outside your company who can help you find the next thing. If you are in a location with active security networking groups, start there. Typically, security people are generous and willing to share their technical skills and their professional connections — use this resource. If you're really ready to make a move from your current role, tell this community. They will be quick to let you know if they hear of new things, and even better, they will likely act as a reference if you need it. If you are a remote worker or are without a lot of local networking groups, use social media to your advantage. Following people on LinkedIn, Twitter, and other platforms will help you make connections that can be used to increase your knowledge and increase your marketability when you're reaching for the next job.

Consider Certifications

If you don't know what role you want next, what certification should you have? Consider getting general industry certifications — CISSP from ISC2, CISM from ISACA, or even a cloud security certification from CSA. Avoid getting an alphabet soup of certifications — too many would indicate that you're not actually applying the knowledge you've gained. However, having a couple of core certifications is a good way to open doors or to be ready when someone opens a door for you.

Be careful — not all certifications are considered equal. (For more detail, check out Chapter 4, "What Training Should I Take?") Sometimes, you can get certified simply by taking a test. For other certifications, you need five years of experience. Even if the certification requires work experience, preparing for and passing the exam is worth putting on a résumé because it can signal that you've done your homework and are ready for a role in that area.

If funds are a problem, there are online training, books, or other lower-cost options to learn the materials. Also, check out your local security organizations, such as ISSA.org or ISACA.org. Sometimes, they offer cheaper preparation classes than some of the for-profit boot camps.

Do You Need a Graduate Degree?

People who are a few years into their career, with a bachelor's degree already in hand, often come to a place where they consider whether a master's degree would be useful to help with career progression. As with all things in security, there is no right answer. If you are looking to get into a senior leadership position, having a master's degree can help, although it's not often required except in select industries.

If you are going to pursue a graduate degree, balance the subject with your undergraduate major. For example, if your undergraduate degree is not in technology, consider a master's degree that at least focuses on technology. If your undergraduate degree was technology-based, consider a general business degree. For those in the policy and governance functions, degrees in policy or law could be a useful investment.

Use the graduate degree to round out your résumé and demonstrate leadership for promotions.

The Intentional Career Seeker

Some have a definite security path they want to follow. They want to be a CISO or they want to be a security researcher or they want to be . . . well, whatever they want. For these people, they get to specialize and specialize early. (Of course, maybe their goal is to be a generalist — in which case, see the previous discussion.)

If you know what you want, then chasing it can mean following this path:

- **Find someone already in that role:** If you can create a mentor or advocate relationship with them, great. (Just ask. You'd be surprised how many senior leaders would say "yes" to a direct request.) If not, at least check out their work history. How did they get to where they are? What education did they earn? What professional experience do they have? What kinds of projects and assignments did they take? If you know what they did, you can choose to intentionally replicate some of their career to get you to the same place.

For example, a hypothetical CISO will have the following background: 10 to 15 years of experience in security, some time in general technology, experience leading multilayer teams, deep experience in two or more security disciplines, experience in two or more industries or subindustries, and experience leading major/large projects.

You're going to have to get creative. The technology and opportunities that a CISO had through their careers from the 1990s to the 2020s won't exist in the same form for you, particularly if you're just starting out. So, be prepared to translate a career experience that happened to someone else many years ago to your opportunity and environment today. One way to do this is to look at someone who is halfway to the role you want. For example, if a CISO becomes a CISO by having managerial experience, find someone who is a new manager, and work out how they got there. Their experience becoming a manager will be similar to yours because of the timing.

- **Know the knowledge and skills that role requires:** Check out job postings to see what skills are currently required for the role you're chasing. Read a lot of them. (Some hiring managers are awful at writing job postings, so don't take one posting as a definitive list of requirements; take a general sample of multiple postings.) Pay attention to skills that are required versus those that are optional. Also, pay attention to the skills that are not specifically security skills, such as teamwork, writing, and general communication. These are as important, if not more important, than the security skills and are the most transferable to other roles.

We are starting to see resources for job hunters and hiring managers, such as the NICE Framework (https://niccs.us-cert.gov/nice-cybersecurity-workforce-framework-work-roles) or Cyberseek.org. Here, you can learn what kind of skills and experiences different jobs require. Be careful, however, as these sites are still being developed. Validate your findings with your network. Still, they can be a benchmark against which you can measure yourself.

Compare Yourself, Part 1

Take a look at your own résumé. What is already on your résumé that will help get you to your desired role? If you already have some skill/experience, don't go looking for something similar. Think of your career like a brick wall; each brick is a skill or experience, and you need to add them in until you have the wall (role) you want. Don't keep replacing similar bricks on the wall, though, because that won't help achieve your plan. For the skills or experience you are lacking, pay attention to the things that are closest to your existing experience, and see what you need to do to bridge the gap between the two. That will be your next step.

Compare Yourself, Part 2

Know your strengths (things that energize you) and likes. (For a general inventory, consider reading *Now, Discover Your Strengths* by Marcus Buckingham and Donald O. Clifton.) Layer your security skills on top of your strengths. Look for roles and projects that leverage your strengths and play to the things you like. For example, if you enjoy teaching others, find roles that give you the time to do that kind of work. Alternatively, don't attend to your weaknesses by taking on an official role that focuses on those things. Instead, look for extracurricular ways of filling in the gaps. For example, if you're not a great public speaker, don't look for a job that requires a lot of public speaking. Instead, consider doing individual training or joining groups like Toastmasters to help minimize those weaknesses.

As you work your way through your career path, you might find that the things you like and are good at have nothing to do with the ultimate job you're seeking to obtain. Be prepared to change your goal if you find that your strengths and likes don't match where you are headed. In other words, be flexible. There are plenty of ways to be a leader in security without being a chief information security officer (CISO). There are plenty of ways to be a subject-matter expert without being a chief architect. Remember that you want to be successful in your career, not burned out and unhappy. Know yourself and act accordingly.

Throughout your career, there might be some mix of being opportunistic or intentional; you generally know which way you want to head (intentional), but you might not know exactly how to get there (opportunistic). Or perhaps you are just bored and looking for a change (opportunistic), but you definitely know what you don't like (intentional). All of that is to say, working in security provides lots of options, and having self-awareness will help you take advantage of those options. So invest time, intentionally, in yourself.

How to Get Promoted

For many people, getting promoted seems like a dark art with a secret code only a few are privileged to know. As much as companies try to provide career ladders and resources for progression, promotion opportunities cannot be totally controlled by the individual. They come about when a company needs a person in a higher role, you are ready to take it, and your manager is ready to support your promotion. There are steps you can take to improve the likelihood of promotion.

- **Apply outside your company:** Let's get this out of the way first. Many security professionals advance their career by moving to another company to take a higher role. It's certainly a strategy to pursue and will often be the fastest way to advance. It may also come with a greater compensation package than an internal promotion would provide. Be careful not to hop too often, particularly as you get into more senior roles. Be prepared to stay in a role for at least a couple of years before moving to a new company.
- **Talk to your manager:** Let them know that you are interested in a promotion, and ask them what it will take to make you ready. They might have coaching for certain skills or experiences you will need. They might think you're ready now but don't have a role available. Knowing where you start is valuable. Letting your manager know you want a promotion is a good seed to plant. They might have already been considering you for a promotion — but perhaps not. Your conversation and request for guidance will encourage them to consider your candidacy seriously.
- **Find a sponsor:** A sponsor is someone in your company who will advocate for you and your performance. They will support you as a promotion candidate or recommend you for interesting projects. Typically, a sponsor is someone who is at your manager's level or higher and is in a role that would have input into the promotion process. Sometimes, sponsors can also be mentors, but not always. The reason to find a sponsor is to help you be noticed in a positive light, which positions you for higher roles.

- **Promote your work:** Some people make the mistake of thinking their good work will speak for itself and that no self-promotion is necessary, particularly when it comes to their immediate manager. Unfortunately, this isn't the case. If you are interested in getting promoted, you need to help the people around you see that you are ready for promotion. Make sure your manager and management chain gets regular updates about your work activities — tasks you've completed and thanks you get from other people. Take time during formal review periods to seriously document all you've done to help the team, your manager, and the company. Make sure your work objectives and results align with the team's goals and the company so you can demonstrate business effectiveness. Be vocal in your appreciation of other people. Include their managers in any thank-you messaging. Ideally, they will return the compliment.
- **Look for opportunities in your company:** Not all promotions happen on the same team. Sometimes, the promotion takes place when you move to another function on the team, but sometimes a promotion can occur when you move elsewhere in the organization. Don't wait for your manager to recommend you to that hiring manager. If you see a role that would result in the promotion you are seeking, don't hesitate to apply for it.

What's Next?

- Talk to your manager. Let them know you want to pursue a promotion and ask them for guidance.
- Review how you talk about your work accomplishments. Make sure your manager is getting regular updates.

- Find a sponsor and let them know what your plans are.
- Conduct a skills inventory. Know what you want to build on and where you need to invest time to learn new things.
- Consider your network. If it supports where you want to head, great! If not, consider adding to it.
- If you have skills gaps, find ways to fill them in the next 12 months.

CHAPTER 12

Should I Manage People?

Summary

- **Know yourself:** Be intentional about moving to a management role. Understand why you want to do it and how it aligns with your strengths and values.
- **Network:** Talk to people in management and single-contributor roles. Learn about what they do, how they do it, and how to find people who can mentor you through this next step.
- **Stay curious:** Learn about management fundamentals like coaching, delegation, and giving feedback — *before* you take a management job.

People in security and outside think that a sign of career progression is to manage people — if they are going to progress in their career, they should manage people, too. They think that being a manager confers authority and that more authority means more seniority, which means more money and prestige. Being a manager is a path to career progression. It is not the only path, so don't assume that it is the only way for you to advance.

There is a tendency to see management as just an extension of your existing skills. For example, if you are a good pentester, it's a logical step to run a team of pentesters. Nothing can be further from the truth. Becoming an adequate manager takes specific training and on-the-job learning. It is a completely different skill set than anything else you've done, and unless you devote time to becoming a good manager, you will be a bad one — and that is hard for everyone around you.

Most people who land a management role receive no management training beforehand. Think about that for a second. The most influential role in an organization is given to people with no previous training or experience, and then we find out if they can do the job. Why do we do this? It's not fair on the manager, and it's certainly tough on the people they manage. There seems to be a school of thought that suggests if you can manage yourself (to a high performance), you can somehow manage others. Any parent will tell you that unless someone wants to be managed, they will not do what you tell them to do simply because you tell them. Some of us get lucky and find out we have some natural abilities that carry us through the worst of our learning period. Some of us aren't so lucky and go through the arduous task of realizing we're in the wrong job.

We have all heard horror stories of bad managers — the micro-managers, the too-friendly managers, and the not-technical-enough-to-run-a-tech-team managers. We've also heard stories about the good managers — the ones who support their teams, lead with integrity, and know their technologies. We all want to be good managers. The challenge with management is that the judgment of "good" or "bad" often lies with the people being managed — and they all want different things. Some employees want a coach, some want a friend, and some want a taskmaster. You quickly learn that managing people means not being able to satisfy everyone simultaneously, which can be difficult at best.

If you are thinking about moving into a management role, slow down and really think about why you want to do it and why now. The stakes are high, so make this move intentionally and with a full understanding of the path you are committing to.

Leadership and Management

A person is a leader when they influence others. Whether you are a single contributor or a manager, you can choose to be a leader. You don't need to have formal administrative authority over a team of people to be a leader in your team, organization, or community. People chasing a career often rush to get to their first management role, thinking it will make them a leader. It doesn't. Instead, it gives them more responsibility to make other people get stuff done, and they quickly realize that the amount of gravitas they receive is far outweighed by the workload. Anyone in any role can be a leader. Anyone can influence others, can direct a team, and can make positive changes.

Alternatively, it can help to be a good manager if you have some leadership skills. That is, if you can understand how your employees think, work, and are motivated, you can influence them to higher performance. You still need the management skills of organization, task management, technical understanding, and so on, but your leadership tendencies will help.

This overlapping relationship between leadership and management can make it easy to confuse leadership and management. Don't let it.

There are a few times throughout a career that are truly momentous — the times when you can see a "before" and an "after." One of those times is making the switch from being a single contributor to managing a team of people. How do you know if you should be a manager or a single contributor? Let's consider the options discussed in the following sections.

What Is a Single Contributor?

In security, we all start as single contributors while we hone our technical skills. But there are several career paths that can take you beyond entry-level learning into leadership without managing a team. Not all roads lead to being a CISO. Security architects, ethical hackers, security researchers, and security product management are all examples of roles that don't automatically assume running a team. Being a technical expert provides enormous value to an organization, and these roles are demanding and come with high responsibility and high salaries.

Single contributors love the technology, analysis, activities, and outcomes, and they want to focus on those things much more than spending time driving other team members' work. This doesn't make them an introvert, a bad team member, or a loner. It just means that their own work is the primary focus of their job.

To be a single contributor leader in security, a person needs to be constantly learning, constantly networking, and comfortable with influencing others without needing direct authority. Single contributors who are leaders often have several years of experience in security and typically lots of years in a single functional area. "Self-directed" and "self-motivated" are often-used phrases to describe single contributor leaders — and for good reason. Often, they have developed technical chops that take them way beyond other leaders in an organization — so if they're going to continue to progress, they will need to find their own paths. They will also have to be a vocal advocate for where to head next. Their managers won't know where to send them. Single contributors don't wait to be told what to do and where to go. They make their own way.

It is a great idea to focus on being a single contributor if being a manager leaves you cold. Look at what your current manager does (and other company managers do). Imagine yourself doing that. Does it seem boring or stressful? Look at the single contributor leaders in your organization (even the non-security ones). Does it seem interesting? Energizing? Exciting? Having a manager title can be gratifying if you are looking for status — but the work happens on a minute-to-minute, hour-to-hour, day-to-day, month-to-month, and year-to-year way. If you don't like the minutia of management work, you will not be successful.

What Is a Manager?

Security management happens when you have a team of people doing similar work, and the team needs someone to guide its work output. The size of the team will vary based on lots of factors — the company's overall size, the organizational philosophy of the company (hierarchical or flat), the repetitive nature of the work, and so on. Few organizations plan out how the organization will grow. Growth happens organically, so management roles arise organically, too.

If you're going to manage people, you need to want to work with people. (I know, this sounds self-evident, but I've bumped into more than one person who realized too late that leading people meant dealing with people issues when they thought it was something else.) You must be interested in investing your time in your staff as your primary obligation. The measure of your success is how well the team does, not how well you do individually.

Just like the rest of security, you will want to be constantly learning, constantly networking. You will need to influence without authority, *and* you will need to be able to influence your own team directly. When you step into a management role, you accept that you will learn about managing people, which means you will have less time to spend on your own deep technical learning. You will accept that progress and development of a team takes longer than simply working on your own, so you will need to be comfortable with longer and more complicated timelines for delivery and success. You will also benefit from having a team of people to delegate to, to share the workload, and whose output is often greater than the sum of their parts. In other words, with a team, you can amplify your influence more than you can as a single contributor — if you have the skills to make that happen.

As employees, we see our manager as the person we work with one-on-one, and of course, your issues are meaningful. But when you're a manager, you have multiple staff issues, not all of them meaningful to you, and you have to share your energy across your entire team. You must be available to your team all the time, and they will have problems as unique as they are. To be a good manager, you will need to put your team's needs before your own, as well as your own technical priorities.

The worst kind of manager is someone whose primary goal is to make other people like them. This personality trait stops the manager from making difficult staffing decisions and leads to bad teams and bad outcomes. If you are a person who wants to be friends with everyone all the time, don't be a manager.

It will create stress for you when you need to reprimand or performance coach one of your team, or worse, fire them. As a manager, you want mutual trust and respect. Still, you must be able to separate your management decisions that might be difficult for your staff to hear (even if it's in their best interest) from your desire to maintain a friendship.

When thinking about management, some people think management is great because you have status, have more control, and get to set the team's direction. All those things are true, but management is also about putting other people first; it's about administrative work, following processes, budgeting, and other administrative things. Make sure you're ready and willing to do all that kind of work!

Middle Management — The Blended Role

A word of warning: if you take the step from being a single contributor to being a middle-level manager, you should know that this kind of role is one of the most difficult to do. Why? Because the role is often a blend of having technical/operational responsibilities *and* being a team manager. It is a role where you will be evaluated both for your individual technical outcomes as well as the success of your team as a whole.

This is a difficult balancing act. On the one hand, you will have your own personal deliverables and activities. On the other hand, you will have staff who rely on you for guidance, direction, and coaching. Their needs will come before your own — but you will still be accountable for your own delivery.

Another challenge is that your staff might pressure you to make changes that you can't always make because you don't have enough authority to influence upper management. Sympathizing with your team may make them like you, but doing so might also make you appear ineffectual. You are stuck in the middle.

If you find yourself in this kind of role, learning to prioritize and delegate are the critical skills you need to learn first. Being able to prioritize the important over the urgent, delegate the less-important work to more junior members, and leverage the power of the team to achieve group goals will all make your life easier. Be prepared for this kind of challenge in "middle management" roles.

Preparing for Your Next Role

The stakes are high. If you move to a management role and are a bad manager, you're not only impacting your own career, but you are affecting the careers of those you manage. Becoming a manager doesn't have to be the way to authority. Taking the time to be ready for management is important.

Don't feel pressured to take on a manager position as a way of advancing. If this is the only way to move up in your company, but you have decided to take a single contributor path instead, look for senior positions elsewhere. Another option is to talk to your management/HR department about creating a more senior role that doesn't require people management. "Moving up" can mean a change in compensation, title, benefits, perks, and a broader or deeper responsibility. For example, instead of engineering for a single tool or system, engineer for a platform of tools. Instead of doing governance, risk, and compliance (GRC) for a single location, do it for multiple locations. Instead of doing something for a single part of the organization, do the same thing for multiple parts of the organization. You get the idea. If you expand your scope and influence, you take on the increased leadership, visibility, and responsibility without taking on people in an administrative capacity. Consider reading *What Got You Here Won't Get You There: How Successful People Become Even More Successful* by Marshall Goldsmith.

If you want to "try on" management stuff before taking a management role, look for job roles where you must influence other people. For example, try leading an important initiative or project, mentoring or coaching more junior people who don't report to you, or volunteering with external security organizations to run an event. These are ways to learn how to coach, encourage, and manage other people, even if you don't have the manager title. Read *The Manager's Path: A Guide for Tech Leaders Navigating Growth and Change* by Camille Fournier.

Before deciding to shoot for a manager role, talk to other managers at your office. Ask them what their day looks like. Ask them about how they manage their staff and what they do when an employee isn't performing well. Ask them what they like and don't like about their job. Ask them what kind of support they get from their manager, human resources, or the rest of the company. As you hear their answers, think about whether you would like what they like and if you would like to do what they do.

Whether you double down to become a more senior single contributor or take a step toward management, either role is a new phase in your career. No longer are you the junior resource who is subject to lots of oversight and who has little autonomy; now, you are a formal manager/leader who is making your own decisions and is accountable for the results. One of the reasons managers make more money is their decisions can positively or negatively influence the outcome of the entire organization. Don't take this responsibility lightly. It can be tremendously rewarding and stressful. Go into it with your eyes wide open.

What's Next?

- Find a manager or two and interview them about their jobs. What is the job like? What do they do to manage people? What do they like or not like?
- Find a senior single contributor or two, and interview them about their jobs? What is the job like? What do they do? What do they like or not like about working with teams?
- Find classes on management, coaching, and influencing, and take a couple. Does the topic interest you?

CHAPTER

13

How Can I Deal with Impostor Syndrome?

Summary

- **Check your thinking:** When you start to doubt yourself, step back and do a dispassionate review of your work and outcomes.
- **Network:** Whenever self-doubt appears, find trusted partners with whom you can check in.
- **Act quickly:** Don't let your worries fester. Reach out to mentors and friends to double-check your thinking.

- **Communicate well and often:** Keep track of your accomplishments. Use this to talk to stakeholders about your job; also, this will help remind you of the good work you do!

When people are new to a profession or come in as entry-level people, they rarely deal with the anxiety of expectations because they expect to know very little. They expect that people around them will be tolerant of lots of questions and lots of mistakes. The anxiety that is commonly labeled "imposter syndrome" starts to emerge when someone presents themselves as an experienced professional, a subject-matter expert, or a leader. When they must prove their bona fides to themselves and others, they might start to question themselves.

More than other parts of the technology world, security has a certain culture, and we're proud of it. This culture is a blend of technological brilliance, countercultural subversion, and savior complex. There is also a hierarchy — it seems that technology programmers and hackers are on the top of the heap, and risk governance and administrative control management are somewhere at the bottom. The hierarchy shifts from industry to industry and from time to time, but a hierarchy remains.

People might come into the profession as a single contributor using their technical skills, and as they gain more experience and do more management stuff, they find themselves using less of their security technology gifts and more of their organizational skills. Because a manager uses fewer technology skills, they have to work harder to stay in touch with the core security culture. The feeling of falling behind and needing to work harder to maintain relevance contributes to their general anxiety.

For most of us, this means that no matter where we are in our security career, there is a tendency to second guess ourselves.

Am I technical enough? Am I working in the right kind of security? Do I belong here? Should I be doing more or something else? The very nature of security work encourages us to question the authority and integrity of the technology and systems we support, and we often turn that critical lens on ourselves. This leads to a fear that we're a fraud and that someone will discover that we're really not the security professional they thought we were.

No one walks around in a constant state of performance anxiety. But, for most of us, there are certain situations where we are more likely to feel it. We often succumb to impostor thinking whenever we talk to someone with more technical knowledge, experience, or confidence than we have — which is a lot of people and a lot of the time! We feel it when we're presented as a subject-matter expert (SME) when we know full well we don't know everything and that someone else knows more. It's an uncomfortable first-reaction feeling.

My Story

When I was new to working, new to working in technology, and new to working in security, I didn't suffer from impostor syndrome. I knew that I knew not much about anything, I knew I had a lot to learn, and I knew that other people knew that, too.

My first inkling of anxiety about my legitimacy started when I became a manager. I was not promoted to manager because of my technology skills; I was promoted because of my human interaction and strategy skills. So, here I was managing a small group of technologists. Who was I to tell them what to do? Who was I to be made their manager when they knew so much more than me? Maybe I got the promotion because they didn't know what else to do with me? Maybe I got the promotion because I was a woman, and they wanted a diversity hire? The rational part of my head always argued against this narrative — you're good at what you do; the role of a manager requires different skills; and if they didn't want you, they'd fire you. However, I couldn't help but let that little voice nag me every once in a while.

The second wave of impostor syndrome happened when my role required me to influence, cajole, and flat-out require that people be more secure and manage risk my way. Who was I — with my nontechnology degree and lack of geek credentials — to require anyone to do anything? When would executive leaders find out that they'd backed the wrong horse? When would my recommendations lead to a catastrophic outage or, worse, a breach?

When things were going great, when I was getting lots of positive feedback and projects were being delivered on time, and when board presentations were well received, the little voice in my head got quiet. When things were not so great, partners pushed back, team members second-guessed my decisions, or I received negative feedback about my performance, the little voice would get louder. Do I really belong here? Who was I kidding by pretending to know what I'm doing? Why should anyone listen to me anyway?

Over the years, I've learned that most of us are touched with a bit of impostor syndrome every so often. I would argue that it's healthy to have a bit of self-doubt — it forces you to reflect on your own performance and ultimately makes you stronger. But too much impostor syndrome is insidious, is damaging, and causes good people to leave the industry. As I talk to people across all parts of our industry, most own up to having their own version of imposter syndrome.

Impostor syndrome affects almost everyone in multiple industries. In security, it occurs throughout the profession. It can impact women and minorities to a greater degree than others because they are already working harder to exist in the culture.

So, what can we do about it?

Fact-Check Your Inner Monologue

When you feel a bout of impostor syndrome coming on, the first thing to do is step back and dispassionately review the situation. Are you responding to a single comment or a range of feedback? Going through a stressful time that makes all things more difficult? Are you feeling less than adequate in comparison to someone else's success? Be clear with yourself about what is driving the feeling of inadequacy.

Be balanced in your examination. Look at your track record. Are your doubts reflected in your work outcomes? Are you generally successful and the current anxiety doesn't match your feelings? Or is your work suffering, and there might be some legitimacy to your thoughts? Think of the people you trust — what messages are you hearing from them? Do their comments match your concerns?

Are you being fair to yourself? No one is exceptional all the time — not even the superstars in our industry. Do you expect perfection from your team, or are you holding yourself to a higher standard than everyone else? What's happening in your personal and work life right now? Is your total life experience helping or hurting your work outcomes? Is your environment supporting your work or hampering it? It's a balance. High goals can be motivating. They are also a recipe for disaster if you set the goals to a level that cannot be realistically achieved. Work with your manager and peers to validate that you're finding the sweet spot, and allow for life to happen, which means sometimes you won't hit the goal. And that's just part of being a good security professional.

Consider who the comments are coming from. Sometimes, a comment about your performance can come from someone without a full understanding of your work or reflect bias from the person giving the comment — intentional or not. If a piece of your brain thinks this might be the case, again, check in with trusted partners. How can you frame the feedback in the context of someone who might be ageist, sexist, or racist? Regardless of bias, should you act on the feedback anyway?

Often, a period of reflection is enough to remind yourself that you are doing just fine, that everything is okay, and that you're enough. Sometimes, you might have a lingering concern. You then have to go a little deeper.

Know Competence and Incompetence

This is a hard one, particularly at the beginning of your career. There are certainly a lot of spectacular professionals to look up to, and you don't yet know enough to be able to judge who is truly competent and who just does great marketing. Time will reveal it.

In the meantime, know what competence looks like for *your* role in *your* company and *your* industry. There is no job in security that requires you to know everything about everything — and yours is no exception. Every part of your job, or any job, can be broken down into skills. And for every skill, there is a continuum of mastery. When you learn a skill for the first time, you make lots of mistakes, and it takes time to become competent. This is true for any new skill, even if you have lots of years of professional experience. It takes even more time to become a master. Just because you have been in your role for a couple of years or more doesn't mean you can be a master at everything, so if you think you should be, please reset your expectations!

Talk to your boss, your colleagues, and your friends, and judge for yourself if you are doing your job well. This doesn't mean being an expert in everything in your field (unless the job title is "security expert"!). However, it does mean that there will likely be areas you can improve, and you should proudly and actively work on that improvement. By the way, *proudly* doesn't necessarily mean shouting it from the rooftops. It can mean quietly owning your own learning path and working it.

Remember that there is more to competence than technology skills — even at the beginning. The best employees are low drama, highly collaborative, quick to help others, and generally able to see beyond themselves. Being competent in your role means being curious and learning quickly, working well with others, communicating effectively, and being reliable. The technology skill is important, but it's not the only ingredient. Don't forget to pay attention to competency in those other areas as well.

If you've assessed yourself, you've gotten feedback from people around you, and you think you're doing the right things, then great! You might find there are some areas that need some work. Now that you are aware of it, you can do something about it.

Know When to Ask for Help

Always start by asking people around you, in your immediate company, for assistance. They know your environment better than anyone else and can guide you most effectively to be successful in your current role. They know the culture of the company, as well as the tools and processes you must follow. It is, after all, up to your immediate company to evaluate your work performance.

If you're not comfortable asking co-workers for help (that's a red flag about your company culture if that's the case) or if there is no one in your immediate company who can help with your skill deficit, then consider the broader security community. Ask questions on Twitter or other social media sources and meet with others one-on-one who are willing to talk about a particular problem or concept. This applies to technical knowledge. For example, ask "What are you doing about zero trust?" and "How can I get involved in capture-the-flag (CTF) events?" Also, this applies to surviving-at-work questions, such as "How do you handle it when you think your boss makes a bad decision?" And that leads me to . . .

Keep Learning and Know When Enough Is Enough

If you think you lack a particular skill or experience area, this can be a great topic to get help from a mentor. Ask around for someone who is really great at that skill or has a reputation for being a good teacher in this area. Ask them to take you on as a mentee. The mentorship doesn't have to last forever but can go a long way to help you jump-start any area in which you think you need help. They can also level set to help you know if you really need help or whether it's just impostor syndrome talking.

On the other hand, you can't know everything about everything — so even if a well-intentioned person gives you feedback that makes you think you need to learn more, you also need to be careful about spending time in areas that won't help you in the long run. Some skills take a lifetime to master. Usually, these involve anything working with people. But for technical skills, you need to decide if you've already learned enough and leave it at that. You need to judge this both in terms of your current role and in terms of your *next* role. Would learning this skill make you demonstrably better at what you do now? If yes, then go ahead and keep learning. If the skill would make you better in your role but not necessarily in a way that your company/manager values, then it might not be worth spending time there. Would learning this skill help you in your next role, even if it doesn't do a lot for your current role? If yes, then it still might be worth learning. Before you invest the time in learning more, evaluate the short- and longer-term value of that effort.

Keep Track of Your Successes

One way to keep self-doubt at bay is to keep a list of the things that went right. The list doesn't have to be Big Things like significant projects or solving world hunger. It can be a daily, weekly, or monthly list of positive interactions with peers, deadlines met, and new things learned.

Having such a list is helpful to prevent burnout and to keep your attention on positive things. It's useful to have a list when you meet with your boss; this list should include what worked well, what you are working on, and what you need help with. It's also a great way to remind you of your accomplishments when the seeds of self-doubt start to sprout. Imposter syndrome can be a kind of distorted thinking, such as when you think you are to blame for the challenges of your work or that you don't deserve the successes that you've had. Having a list of accomplishments helps remind yourself that you are doing a good job and deserve to be in your role.

If you are a woman or minority in security, it can also be helpful to keep track of successes for the people with whom you identify. (Check out Valerie Young's *The Secret Thoughts of Successful Women: Why Capable People Suffer from Imposter Syndrome and*

How to Thrive in Spite of It.) For example, I love to see news about other women in security and their successes (and challenges). Of course, their successes have nothing to do with me, but it is helpful to know that a woman *can* be successful in this field, and it helps me not use gender as one of the reasons to think I'm an imposter. Having a list of successes for other people like me can help reinforce my belief that, yes, I do indeed belong here.

What's Next?

- Create your own "brag wall" — even if you're the only one who sees it. Keep track of your successes. Not only does this help when you need to update your résumé or do a performance review, it is also a great thing to pull out when you're feeling like an imposter.
- Identify a friend or mentor you can contact when your imposter syndrome is at its worst. Choose someone who knows you well enough that you trust what they're saying but who isn't so in the weeds of your day-to-day that they can't see your big picture.
- Consider taking time to fact-check yourself when imposter syndrome hits. A quick self-review can show you that your anxiety is not the definitive authority of your worth!

CHAPTER

14

How Can I Know If It's Time to Move On?

Summary

- **Know yourself:** Be clear about what you like and what you don't in your current role. Be intentional about what a different role would need to offer you to make it worthwhile to leave.
- **Are you finished with your current role?:** Have you done all you set out to do? Have you done everything, learned all you need to, gained the experiences that you wanted?
- **Network:** Talk to your manager and others in your company about other jobs and projects you can do to

keep growing. Talk to the security community to better understand opportunities outside your company.

- **Is where you are headed better than where you are now?:** Changing jobs takes a lot of effort. Make sure you're leaving your current role for something worth the effort to change.
- **Communicate well and often:** Let people know you want to grow — from your immediate manager to the broader security community. If they know you are eager to advance/change roles, they'll let you know when opportunities arise and perhaps mention you to hiring managers.

There comes a time in every person's professional life when they wonder if it's time to make a change. Some of us are easily bored, and this feeling arrives more frequently. Some of us are in a role that just isn't working out. Some of us are just done with learning whatever the current role has to teach.

There are typically good things about a current job that make it tempting to stay where you are. There is comfort knowing your role, knowing what is needed, and knowing how to get things done. Maybe your team is great to work with, fun to be around, and almost like family. Perhaps there are things you had hoped to achieve that you haven't quite done yet. All good things are worth weighing against the feeling that it's time to leave.

Changing roles is a lot of work. There is résumé updating, interviewing, cleaning up the old job, learning the new job. It changes your professional life, and it also messes with your personal life. Your family and friends are on this journey with you, so you're not just impacting yourself. If you're a manager of a team, you are also leaving behind people who are now wondering who their new boss will be and what it will mean for them now that you're gone.

Eventually, there comes time to make a move out of the immediate team or even the entire organization. The trick is to work out whether you are making a move for the right reason — both why you're leaving and whether you're going to something worthwhile. The answer to this question is as varied as the individual who is asking it, though the way to decide is often the same. The following sections outline some things to consider.

Are You Happy Where You Are?

It seems counterintuitive, but I'm often asked if it's time to move on by people who are really happy in their current positions. They worry that if they stay in one place for too long, they will stagnate, both in technical skills and in career progression. They worry that they'll fall behind in their compensation package (the "incumbent penalty"). They worry that they'll be taken for granted by their company.

It can be hard to find a place where you are completely happy. The health and wellness benefits of being in a place like this are high. So, if you are in such a place, there must be a really good reason to leave. You should consider seeing what the internal growth opportunities are first. Would your current employer be willing to grow your role into a different/new technology area? Would you be willing to take on new team members (if you're a manager) even in a totally different discipline? Can they offer you better training, benefits, salary to stay where you are? Think about *why* you're thinking of leaving and look to find those opportunities in your current company before you go looking for something completely new.

Of course, if you're not happy where you are, then that choice is much easier — start looking!

Have You Done All You Wanted to Do?

Many people don't think about what they do when they get a job — they are just happy to be there in the first place. More junior people take a job because they see it as the next logical step in their career path. Mid-level professionals are often more discerning.

It is worth taking time to think about what you hope to achieve in your current role (best if you do it before you take the role, but even thinking about it while you are in the role can be helpful). Some people take a job where they are hired to create a security program. Some jobs are created by a company to create a new security function. Maybe you were hired to create opportunities for improvement in the security team. Regardless of why the company creates a job, a person can use the role to gain knowledge and experience in a certain technology or process, learn about another industry, or make connections on their way to a bigger job.

If you've done what you came to do, great. Maybe now is a good time to start looking for the next big thing. Don't confuse "doing what you set out to do" with "there is nothing left to do." There will *always* be more work to be done, more improvements to be made, more hills to climb, or incidents to manage. There will always be new technologies to learn, more vulnerabilities to mitigate, more staff to train, and more executives to influence. The amount of work still to do is not a complete measure of whether you've achieved your goals. The thing to check is whether you've done the work *you* set out to do. If not (and particularly if you committed something to your current company), you might want to think doubly hard about whether now is a good time to leave.

Have You Learned All You Wanted?

Many security people start to think about moving on when they feel they've hit a ceiling insofar as learning new skills or having new experiences are concerned. The skills could be technical or professional. Regardless, if they don't feel like they are growing in their current role or growing as fast as they once did, they start to get itchy feet. This is a particularly thorny problem during an economic downturn — companies often start to "save money" by restricting training and conference attendance. Security is a hot job, and there are lots of positions available — but moving to another company might not solve that issue if the new company is also restricting training dollars.

If you like your job but want more training, consider that there are lots of free or low-cost training options available to you. Online training, books, conferences, and networking events are places to go to learn new things. Even a simple internet search will often point you to new ideas or training.

Often, the issue isn't that you can't self-train. Instead, you might feel that the company has stopped investing in you — or you no longer need them for development. If you want to stay where you are but feel like you're not getting the development support you need, start by talking to your manager and HR department (assuming there is one). Think about the kind of training/experiences you want and see if they can provide them. Often, the company won't know what kind of development you need, so advocate for yourself.

Occasionally, I talk to people who are despondent because a beloved mentor has left the company, and this person was their "guru" for all things security. With that person gone, they feel that the opportunities to learn are greatly reduced. In this case, a word of caution. First, moving to another company won't automatically mean that you will find someone to replace your teacher. More critically, as you move through your career, you will find yourself moving from junior student to senior teacher. There will be fewer people ahead of you from whom you can learn. You will need to forge your own path to learning, which is typically where networking comes in.

If you explore all options and still feel like you've reached your professional peak with them, then consider a move.

What Are Your Long-Term Goals?

For people who know what they want to be when they grow up, it can be clear that it's time to move to a new role to ensure progression toward the ultimate end state. Some people want to be a chief information security officer (CISO), recognize that they've got the basics down, and know that now they need a new position offering management skills development. Or, they want to start their own business, but first, they need to learn the sales/marketing side of the security world. They might want to be a thought leader in a particular technology or security discipline and cannot develop that in their current role. If this is you, moving on to a new job can be a great way to keep momentum toward that ultimate vision.

If you don't have specific long-term plans, it's easier to stay where you are (assuming you like your job) and wait for the next opportunity to come along. You can improve your chances of landing an interesting new thing by increasing networking and mentoring activities. The more people know you, the more they'll let you know of potential opportunities. If you don't have long-term plans but don't like your current job, networking and mentoring are still the way to go to increase your chances of finding a good landing place.

Are You Being Pigeonholed?

Some people get so good at their job that their managers don't want them going anywhere. They get passed over for new positions or new assignments. Even if their managers are compensating them well, that might not be satisfying.

I would encourage conversation with existing management to let them know your desire for growth. Make sure you haven't landed in a place where you are a single point of failure — the only person who can do what you do. When this happens, managers sometimes don't know how to help you with succession planning, so they keep you where you are. Advocate for sharing your knowledge with others so your manager knows it is safe to move you to a new role. Share your role with someone else to free you up to do other things.

Sometimes, managers only know their employees for their jobs and don't know about other skills/interests their employees have. If this is you, consider taking on projects/training outside your normal job (if you can afford the time) to hone your skills in other areas and demonstrate this learning to your manager. Remind them of the other parts of your experience and indicate a need to incorporate those skills into your current role.

If you have a mentor or advocate in your company, ask them for help advocating for you for a different position. Sometimes, a manager will act if a peer or senior leader suggests it to them, so don't overlook this angle.

If your manager cannot accommodate your needs, it might be time to look around for better options.

Do You Fit Into the Culture?

Even in the best of jobs, it's possible to find yourself in a place where the organization's culture and values don't align with your own. Maybe it didn't start out this way, but then there was a merger, a leadership change, or your manager changed. Maybe you changed, experienced a significant life event, or learned new ways of doing things. Maybe you took the job without thinking about the organization's culture and values, and now you're here trying to make it work.

This can be tough—you might like your team, the day-to-day work, and the perks of the job, but at the end of the day, you still go home feeling a bit stressed and a bit dissatisfied. Maybe daily interactions are challenging. Maybe you feel some microaggressions don't mean much individually, but they add up to a feeling of "otherness" and lack of belonging.

Even if a job looks great on paper and people tell you you're lucky to have it, it will always be a struggle if the job doesn't match your personality and values. You can be successful in your role, but the energy you have to expend for that success outweighs the success itself. You'll probably notice that you experience more negative stress than positive stress. Your general health will likely suffer from poor diet, lack of sleep, and elevated cortisol levels. If you can't get behind the company mission, if you disagree with the way management makes decisions, or if you have to put your game face on before you enter the office, then it is probably time to look for other options.

If you find yourself in this predicament, don't stay in it for too long. This is one area where you should act as quickly as possible to change your circumstances. The cumulative effect of having a mismatch of values/cultures is insidious and will contribute to poor performance. Act as soon as you can to make a change.

Job Hopping

Traditional career advice would warn against moving around from job to job too often. There would be questions raised if you jumped every year into a new job. If you are thinking about moving to a new role, it's worth considering how long you've been at your current company. If it's less than a couple of years, you'll need to be prepared to explain why you're ready to move to a new job right now. If you have back-to-back jobs of less than a couple of years, you should really explain that too.

A person who jumps companies too often might be a poor judge of character — their own, or the companies they work for. Such a person might get bored easily or has switched jobs often for some other concerning reason. Of course, it could also mean that companies have experienced layoffs, mergers, or some other thing beyond your control. In any case, it can be seen as a red flag by hiring managers. You might want to use a cover letter or some other indicator to show why your decision to move quickly from company to company is good.

In a bigger company, you can take more opportunities to move around. The company knows your history and can know why you're moving from role to role without a lot of concern. If you are early in your security career, there is an expectation that you will move more often because you are still working out how to work in the industry. It doesn't take much effort or time to move from an entry-level role to a junior role to a mid-level single contributor role, particularly in a company with a structured career ladder. Once you have hit the five-year mark, that progression tends to slow down a bit, as your skills need time to develop through experience. It is no coincidence that most certifications require five years of practical experience.

Of course, all that goes out the window if you're a CISO. The average tenure of a CISO is about 24 to 48 months!

Are the Other Options Better than Your Current Job?

It's easy to get distracted by the bright and shiny opportunities happening elsewhere in security. There are lots of jobs out there (if you're willing to move to take them), and lots of them sound amazing. Assuming you're leaving your current job for a good reason (and before you jump to greener grass), stop to consider whether the job you are going toward is better than the one you're leaving.

Of course, you can start with the benefits package. Don't think about just the salary; consider the whole thing — signing bonuses, retirement, healthcare, parking costs, work-from-home allowances, and profit-sharing. Sometimes, you might take an income cut to find a better job, which is okay. Just do it with your eyes wide open.

Don't forget the other conditions of the job. How often will you need to travel? Do they support the costs of professional certifications and organizational memberships? How many hours a year do they pay for you to take training? What about other employee benefits (gym memberships, discounts, and so on)? What about tuition reimbursements? What are their expectations on work hours — and does this fit your personal life?

What are the longer-term growth opportunities at this company? Can you grow in the role? Would there be other jobs available to you inside the company? Don't go from one dead-end job to another. Make sure you can grow in place.

Double down on learning about the culture. If you can, find people who work at the company and talk to them about what they like and what they don't. Ask about this during interviews. Insider information can be so valuable to make sure they have a good culture fit for you.

When you have all the answers to these questions, take a step back and compare the new job to the existing job. If you still feel it's a better choice, go for it. If your gut is saying to watch out, listen to it.

There is no job that is perfect all the time, and when our current job is difficult, it is often tempting to look for new opportunities. I have no problem with the explorations. It's always good to know what opportunities are out there. But, before you jump, make sure you're leaving your current job for the right reasons and that the new job will be better than the old one.

What's Next?

- Take time to really think about why you want to leave before you think about the next shiny thing. Make sure that you're leaving or staying for the right reasons.
- Consider whether you can find what you're looking for elsewhere in the current company. Talk to trusted mentors or advisers to see if other opportunities will allow you to stay in place.
- Talk to your security network and consider their advice. What's happening outside your current role that could be good? Is that better than where you are?

PART III

Leading Security

Congratulations, you're now leading a security team. Welcome to the community of people who carry the weight of the security organization on their shoulders!

Your team might be small, covering just a couple of security functions, or it might be large enough to have multiple functions across multiple geographies. You might be leading a security program for a start-up or an established company that is only now investing in security. The fundamentals of security leadership are the same. Only the scale is different.

I created this section to help leaders who are jumping in for the first time and who are trying to find their paths. The good news is that most new leaders are chosen for their roles because they already have most of the skills they need, so it's more of a matter of honing what is already there. In this section, we cover the following topics:

Chapter 15, "Where Do I Start?"

When you begin a new leadership role, there is a way to begin. We talk about how to start and what to do in the early days of your role.

Chapter 16, "How Do I Manage Security Strategically?"

It's easy to stay in the tactical weeds, but you have to resist the temptation. We talk about how to create a security strategy for your program.

Chapter 17, "How Do I Build a Team?"

In this chapter, we talk about growing the security function and where to put your resources.

Chapter 18, "How Do I Write a Job Posting?"

This is a key skill for any security manager.

Chapter 19, "How Do I Encourage Diversity?"

If you are going to have a high-performing team, it must be diverse. We talk about how to do that.

Chapter 20, "How Do I Manage Up?"

Being a security leader means leading your management chain. In this chapter, we discuss how to make that happen.

Chapter 21, "How Do I Fund My Program?"

Here, we discuss ways to find resources to fund your security program.

Chapter 22, "How Do I Talk about My Security Program?"

Communicating is the biggest responsibility of a security leader. In this chapter, we discuss how to do this effectively.

Chapter 23, "What Is My Legacy?"

In this chapter, we evaluate why we do security at all and how we can make a long-lasting impact.

Being a security leader is more than a title; it's a way of thinking and acting that brings the rest of the organization along for the ride. It's about making believers of doubters. It's about being a cheerleader for the security team, not the general in charge. It's about subsuming your own ego for the benefit of others. How do you do this? Where can you go to get help? What land mines should you avoid?

The following chapters will help make sense of the security leadership role.

CHAPTER

15

Where Do I Start?

Summary

- **Know yourself:** Understand what strengths you bring to this role at this time.
- **Network:** Build relationships to get information and to provide support when you need to make organizational changes.
- **Stay curious:** Understand how the company thinks about security and how it manages risk in general.
- **Communicate well and often:** Build trust by asking for help when you need it.

When you start a new security leadership role, it can be daunting to know where to begin. There are lots of people, lots of security threats, and lots of business processes. It's tempting to want to jump in with both feet, but try to resist this urge. Going in with preconceived ideas of running or fixing things will inevitably lead to misunderstandings, ruffled feathers, and a lack of trust. Instead, take the time to learn the company, listen more than speak, and build relationships to help create the scaffolding that will support you in the future.

In the beginning, you're trying to answer a simple question: what will it take for you to be successful?

What's on Fire?

Sometimes, before you even walk in the door, you might notice things that need immediate attention. Perhaps they've never had a security leader before, and you can see that they need basic blocking and tackling, such as multifactor authentication for critical systems, vulnerability management for internet-facing assets, or basic asset inventory. Perhaps they are missing some critical security thing that is needed for basic compliance. Perhaps the existing security team is leaving in droves.

If you've been brought into the company in response to a major breach event, your mandate to act is clear and immediate. In this case, you have no choice but to start acting immediately, even if you don't yet have all the facts.

Some things are just glaringly obvious to address right away. Do it. Leverage your relationships with your immediate manager and the people who hired you to get started on those things. Anything else can wait. Once you've taken care of immediate business, then you can get to the rest.

What Is Your Timeline to Act?

I'm a big fan of the book *The First 90 Days* by Michael D. Watkins, which guides a leader through the work of taking on a new role. If you are a newly minted security leader, think about the timeline you have.

You could set the timeline to support your personal goals. For example, you might go into a job thinking you'll only be there for a specific amount of time to learn something, work with someone, or learn an industry. The company might set the timeline: an upcoming audit, the company going public, or a merger or acquisition timeline. And if there are no hard personal or operational timelines, then perhaps your timeline is set by the company's culture. Maybe they expect you to move fast and make changes. Maybe they want you to take your time to learn the business before making any major moves.

The average tenure of a CISO is surprisingly short — between eighteen months and three years. If you are working on this timeline, expect to put in a lot of hours to make changes happen quickly. Accept that you might not be able to do everything that needs to be done. Your role will be to create the beginning of something or fix a problem, but it's probably not to leave a legacy of culture change. Plan your time accordingly, and make sure you are clear on your priorities.

If you have a bit of extra time to spend, you have the luxury to slow down a bit and do some more analysis and relationship building before you act. You will have the time to try things out and experiment with new people, processes, and security tools. You will also need to spend time and effort maintaining the company's focus on security over a longer period.

Whatever your timeline is, as you proceed to evaluate the rest of the organization, keep it front and center in your mind. It will change how you prioritize your own work, your team, and your program.

Who Are Your Partners?

Your success or failure as a security leader will depend on your ability to build relationships inside and outside the security team. It is never too soon to start identifying who your partners, mentors, and stakeholders are. As you meet people, you will quickly learn who is positioned to help or hinder your work, who can become your confidant, and who is a connector who can help you influence the rest of the organization. Be intentional about cultivating these relationships early.

Get to know people personally. Nothing builds relationships faster than by finding out the personal stories of people around you. What's their personal story? What are their hobbies outside of work? What do they care about? What is their family situation? What do they do at work? What are their work priorities?

A security leader must be seen as a trustworthy person, leading a trustworthy team. People are inclined to be trusting, which is helpful. You should start your new role intentionally building your reputation as someone who can be a trusted partner, advisor, and manager. If you start any other way, it will make your longer-term goals much harder to achieve.

- Take time to get to know people and let them get to know you.
- Give them early opportunities to see that you deliver on your commitments, you know what you're doing (even if it doesn't feel like it yet), and you can be relied on to do what you say.
- Don't be afraid to ask for help. This will allow people to know that you are transparent and collaborative.
- Provide people with information about security that is appropriate to their role. This will set you up to be a trusted advisor and thought leader.

Your partnerships will be the things that will make or break your success in your role. Start working on these before you even begin the new job.

Find the Strengths and Note the Weaknesses

When you start thinking about becoming a security leader, you will begin evaluating the company before you even start the job — either as an internal employee or during the interview process. The strengths of a company are easy to see — people will tell you about them. They'll talk about where funding comes from (or not), leaders they like, processes that work (and those that don't). People love to talk about the things that work, and you will learn quickly where the organization can help you. Some weaknesses might be obvious, such as not enough trained staff or poor technology currency, for example. Some weaknesses might be harder to spot, such as toxic internal politics, decreasing revenue streams, or inefficient processes. Keep note of the company's strengths and opportunities.

Take the time to learn the business at the macro level. How does it operate on paper and in practice? How do you get things done in this organization? What ways of working or thinking can you use to further your security objectives? Move fast and ask for forgiveness later? Build a business case and get it approved? A tendency to use external resources instead of in-house? A preference to develop and promote from within? You won't find any of this in an employee onboarding package. You will only learn this by meeting with people and asking questions.

As you are uncovering these strengths and opportunities, consider your own. How do your strengths complement the strengths of the company? Where are your weaknesses going to be problematic? In short, you need to do a personal analysis, evaluating yourself. What are your strengths and weaknesses? What are the cultural/organizational opportunities and threats? Where can you leverage strengths and opportunities and minimize weaknesses and threats?

This shouldn't take a long time to complete. Every time you talk to someone, you should have another nugget of information to add to your analysis. After a couple of weeks (or even during the interview cycle), you will see some themes emerging that can become the place to focus on from the beginning.

Draw the Business Risk Picture

Always, always, always start with understanding what the business is and does and how your company expresses itself. What is the most important business outcome? Profit? Customer satisfaction? World domination?

If you don't have a clear picture of the "why" of the company, you will be lost.

Once you've articulated this, check in with others (including your immediate team) to sense-check your understanding. It's rarely the case that you can boil this down to a simple sentence (and it is *not* the mission statement!). There are layers of cultural nuance that you need to tease out. Meet with people, officially and unofficially, to get their input.

If you know what the company cares about, consider the environment the company works in. What are the characteristics of the industry? High volumes and low margins? Low volumes with high margins? Highly regulated or unregulated? Local, national, or international? High or low public profile? Publicly traded or privately owned? What external forces will shape how the company operates and within which you will need to run your security program?

Most importantly, evaluate senior leadership (as high up the chain as you can go). Do they understand risk management? Is there an enterprise risk management program, and how does security fit into it? What does leadership consider the biggest risks to be? Is security in the top three? How does leadership respond to risk — invest big and early, or delay and hope the risk doesn't materialize into impact? Leadership often understands the risk is about likelihood and impact but often fails to consider the immediacy of the threat or how quickly they need to act. If your leadership fails to act in time, the rest of the organization won't move quickly either. How do they respond to business-impacting incidents of any kind? Do they have a crisis playbook, or do they wing it? Do they band together or point fingers of blame? There is no wrong answer here — just information for you to know as you set your program and build your team.

Do You Have a Mandate?

When you're interviewing for a security leadership role, it is clear early on what people hope you will do in your new role. That mandate will impact what you need to do in the beginning.

Security Leader Mandates

If You. . .	Quickly Consider. . .
Are to create a security team from scratch	Creating a 12- to18-month roadmap for adding functionality.
Fix a broken security function	Evaluating the people and functions on the team to determine what needs to be nurtured or changed and then making those changes.

(*Continued*)

If You. . .	Quickly Consider. . .
Maintain a well-performing team	Evaluate the team to see if you agree with the assessment. If so, plan your future roadmap. If not, work with stakeholders to make a business case for change.
Grow an existing team	Evaluate the team for places to build upon and create a roadmap for growth.

What's Next?

It's easy to think about "starting with the end in mind," but I propose that you can't get where you are going without first knowing where you are. When someone asks where to start, I suggest that they first identify where they are now so they can then build a strategy to help them get where they want to go. Your timeline will help you think through what is possible and practical to achieve and how to go about leveraging your strengths and the company's strengths to make that happen. Keep in mind that your timeline might need to change as you learn more about the company and its needs.

This isn't about security threats and risks (that comes next); it's about understanding the context in which you'll be asked to operate. So, create an analysis of your personal and organizational strengths and weakness, evaluate the risk management style of the organization, and consider your timelines. You now have enough information to begin.

CHAPTER

16

How Do I Manage Security Strategically?

Summary

- **Know your company:** Be aware of the industry or industries you are working in and the nature of the business.
- **Know yourself:** What is your mandate for success, and how much time do you have?
- **Create a plan:** Consider regulations, threats, business objectives, and budgets. Don't forget training and communications.
- **Network:** Validate your plans with your immediate team and company stakeholders.

- **Stay curious:** Revisit your strategy often and course-correct as things change.
- **Communicate well and often:** Measure your progress, and be prepared to discuss your strategy with everyone constantly.

Strategy and strategic planning are the core work of any leader. A strategist must decide what activities the team or organization is going to focus on, to support the desired outcome of the business. It might seem obvious, but when you're leading a security team, you have to have some intentionality about what you're doing regardless of your title. A security leader who operates without a strategic plan will be forever buffeted by the issues and firefights of the day. Your team won't be able to follow, your partners will be driven crazy with shifting demands, and your organizational leadership will fire you. So, one of the first tasks in your leadership role is to create a proactive strategy. When you start as a security leader, you will owe it to yourself, your team, and your stakeholders, to plant a strategic flag in the ground and say: "We are headed *that* way."

Think of strategy like an old-fashioned road map that has been annotated for your specific circumstances. It describes where you are and where you are going. The amount of time you have will determine how much you will see along the way. The map only generally describes how you will get there. It will tell you to head west, but it might not yet tell you whether you're driving, flying, or walking. The map acknowledges that you don't know everything ("there be dragons") and that there might be detours that will require course correction later in the trip. Ultimately, if you run out of gas, you might not reach your intended destination, and that is okay. The point of a strategy isn't to give your team and partners a detailed itinerary. Instead, the point is to give you and your team some general guideposts — a "choose your own adventure" with constraints around what kind of adventures you're willing to let them have.

There is much more to a security strategy than simply the security tools and services you deploy. You must consider how the overall program is managed, which includes the people and processes involved in making your organization secure. Sometimes, the strategy will include nonsecurity things. This might mean working with HR to improve onboarding/offboarding processes so identities can be better managed. Sometimes, this might mean working with the purchasing department to change their processes to suit security vendor buying cycles better. Think holistically about all the things that can impact your journey — it's not just about the technology.

A security strategy is not a short-term project. It is not a thing that happens in a year. It is never "finished." It is also not a policy. A strategy isn't something that controls your team or your company. It is something that enables them to work toward a bigger goal but leaves room for creativity and ownership within the general strategic outline.

Security has a unique strategy problem. A strategic plan is, by its very nature, long-term. This creates a dilemma for security leaders because our tenure is usually short. This means you will need to decide whether your plan will extend beyond your own tenure or whether you will confine your planning to a couple of years. A criticism of security is that we aren't enough of a business partner — and most of our partners are planning at least three to five years into the future. We will need to find ways to address this disconnect if we are to be taken seriously as business leaders.

There are lots of people invested in your strategy. Boards, executive teams, and your immediate leadership will need to buy into your strategy so you can get funding and air cover. Your team will need to know what you're proposing and why so they can get behind your vision. You will need to constantly talk about your strategy to remind them why you're doing what you're doing. Your strategy needs to make sense to security professionals and the business and community in which you work.

Consider Your Industry

As you begin your environmental analysis, start with the big picture and work inward. This means first understanding what industry or industries you are in.

Consider your company. Is it a retail organization? Finance? Healthcare? Technology? What are the characteristics of the industry? Is it low margin, high volume? High margins, specialized service? Private sector or public? What are the current business issues in your industry? Is it struggling or growing? Is it a national or local concern, or is there an international flavor? Where are the opportunities for the industry, and where are the risks? Answering these questions might mean talking to people in your company to get their take on it. You might choose to look at industry analysis organizations. A simple internet search might help you identify themes. Start creating your industry profile.

As a security professional, you will also have to consider security trends and work out how they might align with your industry and company. Security trends are typically driven by technology trends. You will need to triangulate all of those. For example, right now, a lot of older companies are moving their technology stack to the cloud. This means that the security stack will need to support a hybrid technology environment — on-premises and cloud-based. The security industry is dealing with this by considering zero-trust and Secure Access Service Edge (SASE) architectures. Is your team doing this, too? If not, do you think they should be? If so, are they trained and ready? The basis of your justification for the strategy you pursue will be formed by considering what your company needs, overlaying those needs with security/technology trends, and linking them to your team's capabilities.

Know Your Business Priorities

Your strategy should align with the business priorities of your organization. It is easy to say and hard to do. A new security leader might think the security team's mission is to protect the organization or make it more secure or resilient. As the leader, you must find a path from that security mission statement to the organizational goals of serving customers, supporting mergers and acquisitions, attracting top talent, or whatever you determine the business priorities to be. And not only is it point A (security mission) to point B (organizational objective), but you must also take into account the supporting "how." Be efficient, be inclusive, be first to market, and be whatever the business thinks is important.

Most businesses operate with more than one priority. Generally, they want to make money and improve their share prices, but they might also want to expand into new markets, complete a merger, double their head count, or develop a new product. In bigger companies, you might have multiple lines of business, each with its own priorities. If you're in this situation, take a look at the greatest growth and executive focus areas, and make sure your strategy is aligned with this effort. You might have basic blocking and tackling to do, but make sure you're doing it in the high-growth areas of the company first. This will help show that you understand the business priorities, and it is also more likely to get the resources to support your broader program.

In the beginning, you won't have all the answers, and business priorities and corporate culture change frequently. So, consider business priorities when creating a security strategy, but don't lock yourself into it because it will change. Be prepared to regularly adjust your strategy when it does.

Semper Gumby: Always Flexible

I had a five-year security strategy, and I was very proud of it. I collaborated with business leaders, technology partners, compliance people, and others. It took a few months to put together, and I spent more time working with my communications partners to get it just right.

I documented my "why" and "how" and could tell you where we were headed. Within the strategy, we had yearly projects and goals. Everyone was on board.

Then a worldwide pandemic hit. Our way of working was upended overnight. Our security architecture needed to be updated, but funding was diverted to medical testing and online business process changes.

As a security leader, there was no way I could hold on to the original strategy. We weren't going back to the old ways of work, and I did not yet know what the "new normal" would look like. I had to flex with the needs of the business by accelerating some projects and delaying others. I had to re-examine my assumptions that were the basis of the original strategic plan. I had to set aside work to make sure my team was healthy and whole.

That's okay. Being "always flexible" is a key leadership skill for any security leader, and it makes the leader a more trusted business partner.

Why focus on changing business priorities when creating a security strategy? Because your leadership needs you to show that you understand their priorities, so they can support yours. They need to see common purpose and to consider investing in security programs to be a worthwhile business investment, not just administrative overhead.

Be Pragmatic

The best security leaders are, among other things, pragmatic. They don't sell their strategy using fear, uncertainty, and doubt (FUD), nor do they oversell the likely benefits of a security investment. They are clear-eyed about the strengths and weaknesses of the organization and their own security teams, and they can calmly discuss the likely risks and outcomes of their programs with anyone in the organization. Yes, security leaders need to provide inspiration, but rainbows and unicorns are not a strategy that people will follow. Security leaders make promises they can keep because they must be trustworthy in all things.

It is important to know where the roadblocks are likely to be and create a security strategy around, over, or through them. If you know that you're going to be budget-constrained, you might think about using open-source tools or online free training for your staff. If you know that leadership has other, bigger fires burning, it might not be the time to suggest that leadership should have security objectives written into their annual goals. If you are working in a high-volume, low-margin business, spending all your money on one product that addresses only one type of threat might not make sense. Perhaps investing in a generalist security platform might be an easier "sell." There might be some roadblocks that you just can't ignore — like lack of funding. In that case, find short-term actions to move as far forward as you can regardless of the funding shortage, and include working on that funding roadblock as part of your strategy.

It is also important to know what parts of the organization can be pushed and stretched into the leading edge of your strategy. The threat might be so high for some initiatives that you need to engage the entire organization as quickly as possible. In other words, you want to eat the elephant in one bite. You will need active engagement from senior leadership to make this happen. Alternatively, there might be less time-sensitive — although still important — security projects that require your attention. These kinds of initiatives can be done more slowly. Finding a willing organizational partner to take the lead can show the organization the benefits of your strategy, create smaller quick wins, and build trust.

Create your strategy pragmatically, noting the roadblocks and potential partners who can help you overcome them. Not everything needs to be done right now, as much as you wish it — so be intentional about when you need to accelerate an initiative and when it can be done slowly.

Address Stakeholder Pain Points

The best way to attract supporters for your strategy is to listen to stakeholder pain points and ensure that your strategy actively addresses them. For example, the IT staff might feel stuck between budget restrictions that limit what they can do and auditors who expected more than IT can deliver. In this situation, one security team role is to advocate with senior leaders for more investment in security for the IT teams. Also, the security team should advocate with auditors regarding what can be reasonably expected. With both sides feeling supported, they might be more willing to be on the security journey.

Talk to other CISOs and leaders about the security pain points they have tried to address. There are ones common to the industry, with known ways to deal with the problems. Putting in some fixes to these issues will build trust in your community and garner support for your longer-term plans. The following are some common security pain points:

- Security reviews slowing down software purchasing
- Help-desk tickets for password resets
- Code reviews slowing down application delivery
- Users don't like the multifactor authentication (MFA) experience

Sometimes, the pain point has nothing to do with a security policy, technology, or service. Instead, it has more to do with other business processes, such as inefficient HR onboarding processes, lack of competent asset management, or inadequate budget mechanisms. Don't forget to include these things in your security strategy as well. You might not be the "owner" of the problem, but finding ways to solve those items will help the success of the security program and are worth your time and effort to address.

Demonstrating that you recognize the environment you're working in and aligning your strategy to exist in that reality will go a long way toward generating institutional support for your efforts.

Threats and Vulnerabilities

No security strategy would be complete without consideration of known or predictable threats and vulnerabilities. For the security leader, this means completing an internal and external analysis of trends and events and deciding which threats to specifically target in your strategic roadmap.

There are any number of resources to help you with the external analysis:

- Most industries have their own Information Sharing and Analysis Center (ISAC). ISACs provide a wealth of information about typical attack vectors for your industry.
- Other security professionals in your network can also help. For example, a conversation with other security colleagues or listening to podcasts and other feeds can be great sources of information.
- Industry reports such as the Verizon Data Breach Investigation Report (https://enterprise.verizon.com/resources/reports/dbir/) will give you general and industry-specific trends in threats and attack methodologies.

Your internal analysis should also encompass the following:

- Any existing reporting about security incidents and events. If you don't yet have a security team, look to the IT help desk and other partners to give you a flavor for the kinds of events they handle.
- If your company has cyber insurance, talk to your risk partners or the insurance vendor. They can let you know how they completed a risk analysis to arrive at their current policy, or they can give you general information about the risks and threats they see in the company.
- A review of the technology roadmap for your company will also inform your strategy. Whatever technology your company uses has inherent, specific risks. Your strategy should

ensure those risks are addressed. Get in early on that roadmap. The sooner you can be included in those conversations, the easier it will be to align your security strategy and be seen as a valuable partner.

- Evaluate the security culture at your company by talking to people. Your strategy should explicitly talk to the "people" part of the organization and ensure that people are security advocates, not insider threats. Your analysis doesn't have to be intensely quantitative — a few general conversations will give you a sense of what people think about security and its role in their jobs.

As you consider your threats and vulnerabilities, ensure you are thinking ahead. It's not just about the threats you face today; it's also about the likely threats you will face in a year or more. Your authority as a security leader will be judged on how prepared you are to manage new things, so incorporate some "future-proofing" into your strategy. This could be as simple as sending your team to train on securing new technologies, partnering with product teams to experiment with new security solutions, or doubling down on tabletop exercises.

Rinse and Repeat

Like road trips, strategies need constant care and feeding. While a strategy is a longer-term direction that shouldn't change too much, it is also important to review the strategy to make sure you're still headed in a good direction and the roadmap still makes sense for the business.

External things can happen (9/11, recessions, a big data breach, pandemics, and so on) that can change your original plan overnight. Be prepared for this, and never let an incident go to waste. What would you want to ask for if there was a big event (and why aren't you asking for it now)? What would you do if you didn't have sufficient executive attention before and something happens to get that attention? How might that change your strategy?

More likely, internal business changes (change in leadership, change in budget, or change in technology strategy) will need to be factored into your annual plan even while your overall strategy remains the same. Be prepared to make a regular strategy review part of your regular work cycle. Dust it off regularly (how regularly will depend on the business you are in) and ask yourself if it still makes sense. Be prepared to discuss with all your stakeholders any significant changes you need to make.

The role of the security leader is to be the architect of the business's security program. Every program stakeholder will be looking to the leader to articulate where you're going, as well as why, how, and when. Be prepared to answer these questions — all the time.

Putting It Together

There are several items to consider when drawing up your strategy that will feel tactical, but they need to be incorporated into your strategy.

A Security Framework

A framework ensures that everyone talks the same language and knows what needs to be done. Done well, it also helps to know where the organization has gaps and needs focus. Start by looking at applicable regulations to your organization. There are a million details that go into creating a security framework — policies, laws, regulations, standards, and a balance between "must" do and "should do." This takes time, but it a crucial first step in any organization.

Staff Training

I'm not talking about training people on policy (although that was required, too); instead, I am talking about training IT and other key staff to do their jobs securely. Don't forget to train the security teams on how to approach security according to your strategy. Training IT people creates advocates and allies, so it's important! Training your security team creates loyalty and enables the team to work collectively toward a common goal.

Core Services

If you were building a program from the ground up, where would you start? Perhaps it makes sense to start where regulations require services to exist. Being compliant doesn't make you secure. However, leadership understands when they *must* do something according to a regulation or a contract, and often those things can make a positive difference to a security profile. First, evaluate the security services available to satisfy any compliance requirements and then fill in any control gaps. After that, consider the central security functions — identify, protect, detect, respond, and recover — and make sure you're covering those bases in your core services as well. There will be overlap between the compliance and security areas, so double up where you can.

Metrics and Reporting

Create a plan to enable you to assess and report to senior leadership. Changing a culture to be more security-aware takes time, and having data to show changes is critical. It's never too soon to start. There are multiple ways to track improvements and show progress (more on this in a later chapter), and there is no right way. Aligning the reporting to general business goals and organization structure is particularly useful.

What's Next?

- If you haven't already, start writing down your plan. Mindmaps are a great way to start framing out what you want to include. Once you've dumped everything out of your head and onto the page, look for gaps and errors in thinking. The hardest part about creating a strategy is getting started — the faster you can start sharing your thinking with others, the better your strategy will become.
- Socialize your strategy with your management chain. Use the sessions to sharpen your thinking, clarify your delivery, and respond to any concerns they might have.
- Discuss your strategy with your entire team and invite them to give input. Making the strategy a team event can help build internal champions for the work to come.
- Don't wait for the strategy to be perfect. The overall goal posts won't change often, but the planning details will. Refine it as you learn more, as conditions change, and as your team grows.

CHAPTER

17

How Do I Build a Team?

Summary

- **Know yourself:** Understand what the organization wants from you as a security team leader.
- **Network:** Sense-check your plans with internal stakeholders and external subject-matter experts (SMEs).
- **Stay curious:** Continuously assess how well your functions are performing and what can be done to improve them. Don't be shy to stop doing something that is finished or isn't working well.

- **Communicate well and often:** If you're going to make a change or add a new security function, communicate your plans early and widely.

It's rare to have to create a team entirely from scratch. More often, at least a couple of people are already working together to do some security function, and you are asked to build on it. This is particularly true if you are getting your first management role. Often, the function you are leading already exists, and you've been put in charge of it. You are asked to manage the team — so that's what you do.

For most new managers, your first opportunity to decide what your team should look like comes when one of your existing employees leaves. For the first time, you have the responsibility of finding a replacement. For the first time, you get to think about what you really need in terms of skills. You get to think about what kind of personality would work with the team and what kind of person you value as a team member. It is great to have this kind of choice and be reminded of the responsibility of management. Just know that if you get it wrong, it hurts the whole team.

Replacing an existing open role isn't the same thing as building a team. When you are building a team, particularly one with multiple functions, you have many more choices. Do you add more head count to alleviate a team with too much work to do? Do you create a new role to do something completely different for the organization? Do you move an existing resource into that open space (maybe even a promotion!) and then backfill elsewhere? Being able to make these kinds of choices is one of the best parts of being a leader, and it is the place where you can leave your leadership mark.

Building a team that is used to manage security for an entire organization means thinking about what the company needs, what the team can provide, and aligning the two. Growth in the security team means adding resources to address the needs of the company while also taking the culture of the security team into account. It's a tricky balance. It's also a function of being a leader that is never done. This is one of the ongoing operational things you will do every day. Being a security leader is about constantly evaluating your team. Are we providing needed services? Do we have the skills and talent we need? Are our operational processes working correctly? Do my team managers know how to manage a team? Every time someone leaves my team — which is ideally not too often! — is an opportunity to reevaluate the structure of the team.

I consider team building and team management to be among the most important things you do as a security leader.

It Is About the How

A new security leader must simultaneously work on two related issues: what are the security threats and requirements impacting an organization, and how do I create a team that can best respond to those threats? Creating a security strategy is more often about knowing what threats a company faces, the risk tolerance of the organization, and the tools and services available to mitigate the threats. Building a team follows the creation of a strategy. It is about *how* to implement the strategy — where to invest head count, where to outsource, where to consolidate, and where to sunset. This is a continuous activity for a security leader. There should be an ongoing evaluation of whether you have the right resources in the right places, and you can expect it to take up a significant amount of your leadership time.

It is rare when someone gets to create a security team exactly from scratch. Even if you are currently a team of one, there are already other people in an organization doing "security stuff," including the information technology (IT) staff, human resources (HR) partners, finance partners, and even the chief executive officer (CEO). All these people have a role to play in executing security, so the building of your team should fit into the structures that already exist — at least for now.

First, you need to know why you are there.

Build a New Thing

Maybe this company has never had a security team before and you've been brought in to build the team from scratch. Congratulations! If the company really appreciates what security can do, this could be a really rewarding place. I would suggest being as aggressive as possible in getting what you need. Fill your gaps first, apply foundational security functions, ensure you're supporting business growth, and carry on.

Be prepared to spend a lot of your time hiring the right people to fill the roles. If you are truly starting from scratch, consider employing generalists who can be put into multiple roles quickly before investing in specialists. While you're hiring full-time workers, consider outsourcing or staff augmentation to fill some of the second-stage roles so you can get started with the function without depending on what will likely be a long hiring cycle. Over time, if it makes sense, you can replace third-party contractors with internal hires.

Beware: "Build a new thing" has a close cousin called "just do it." This happens when a company understands it must deal with security but doesn't really know what that means. Maybe they are preparing for an initial public offering (IPO), and the regulators are telling them they must have a security leader and a security program. You've been hired to make the problem go away. This is not an awful thing, but this attitude will create some different challenges. If you find yourself in this situation, you might need to make reporting and communications roles part of your early hiring plan.

Fix a Broken Thing

Maybe you're inheriting a team of security functions that are not well regarded by senior leadership. They need you to "fix it." Perhaps they just suffered a breach or had a close call, so they've decided to make a change to the way they do security. Sometimes you might not know this is the case until you've already taken the job (I hope not!). If you've been brought in to "fix the problem," you will need to spend time evaluating exactly what the problem is before you start to build, and often the problem is multifaceted.

Talk to your leadership first to understand how they perceive the security function. Then, talk to existing security teams and other stakeholders (vendors can be a great resource here) to validate or refute the leadership opinion. Determine what needs to change.

If you come into a team that is considered broken, you will likely find a security team that is unsettled and demoralized. You must quickly evaluate the team and determine whether there is anyone who should be supported to find another role outside the team and how you can invest and support the remaining team members. Move quickly on this question. The longer the security team stays in limbo, the harder it will be to move forward, and the less credible you will appear to your team and leadership.

Continue a Great Thing

Maybe you're being brought in to lead a high-performing team. You are expected to maintain whatever is in place. This is rare.

Security people never feel like they've already got it solved, so there will always be new things to do. It is also a difficult task. A team is high-performing because of a delicate balance of leadership, culture, and process. With a new leader — you — the balance is already upset. You will need to work hard to keep the team performing well.

If the company leadership thinks the security team is great, you can build on that to try new things in addition to what already exists. Now is not the time to radically change what is already there. "New" is fine, but "different" is scary. So, as you build your team, be slow to change the existing structures, even if you think change is needed. Add new things that are needed, leaving the old in place for now. Later, you can modify the old structures when the team and leadership are more familiar with you personally.

Keep Building a Growing Thing

Maybe there is a team already in place, but the organization needs it to be doing more. Given the changes in technology and security, this is where most new leaders find themselves. The work of security is never done, and the security functions are not static, so steady growth is a reasonable assumption to lead with.

Consider the existing talent you already have. Is there someone already on the team looking to move or change? Could they be moved into a new role to satisfy the need for a new product or service? Are there efficiencies to be made in how the team operates to free people up to work on new things? Resist adding new functions until your existing services and functions are solidly supported. Of course, timing will be a factor here. You might need to grow fast to satisfy a business need or have a compliance gap that needs attention. Regardless, do what you can to ensure that any existing function is working well before taking on more.

Things to Consider

Thinking about where to begin and how to make changes can be overwhelming. Fortunately, there are some tried and true ways of going about building your team while taking all your unique needs into account.

Plan for Functions, Not Tools

As I discuss various options in the following sections, I'm intentionally using the word *function* and not *service* or *tool*. Grouping tools into services and services into functions allows you to build a portfolio of functions that have structure and common application across a variety of threats and situations. For example, the function of Identity and Access Management (IAM) is made up of identity creation, access lifecycle management, authentication and authorization, group management, and Active Directory management. Adding IAM to a security portfolio isn't about one service. Instead, it is a group of services that, when combined, allow the organization to pursue a zero-trust initiative; facilitate user behavior analytics for incident response; support an on-premises, hybrid, or cloud-native technology stack; manage threats against domain administrators; and so on. It isn't just about one thing (creating login accounts); it has many values for many stakeholders. In the taxonomy of security, there are many tools but fewer functions. Planning and talking about functions helps you work with stakeholders so they understand how all the pieces of security fit together.

Security Hygiene

You've done your evaluation, and you know the lay of the land. Great! Now, you need to decide what is worth keeping. There will be some core security functions that you should either build first (if you're building a team from scratch) or make sure are functioning really, really well. These are known across the industry as *basic security hygiene* tasks or *foundational security*. Making sure you have these in place gives you the biggest return on your security investment.

The problem is that there is less consensus around what those foundational elements really are than you would think. Current favorites include things like vulnerability management, governance frameworks, and incident response. The truth is, what is considered foundational will really depend on the type of company you're in, and it will be your job to make that call.

Regardless, once you have your foundational list, make sure those functions are running well by ensuring the staff doing the job is well trained and professionally managed. Some of these functions (such as asset management) might not be directly part of your team, but they might be critical to the security program's success. Next, review the cost of the service. Is it efficiently run? If not, should this be outsourced, perhaps? Do you need to replace staff or tools? Assuming you have the right staff and tools, then make sure those teams are well supported. Having one person doing a thing is just a single point of failure. Maybe you could have two people each spend half of their time on it, or you could add additional head count to eliminate the failure point. Don't start adding new stuff until the foundational stuff is solid.

Identify Required Functions

Compliance doesn't equal security. Check. You need the basic things required by law or contract, so this is a great place to start adding functions. Check with your cyber insurance provider. What do they assume you have in place or expect you to have? Knowing the regulations that impact your industry and understanding what the regulations require is a solid basis for a quick business case to add more functions to your team. Once your basic hygiene is in place, the compliance things should come next. (They are often the same thing, but not always.)

Add the "Must Do" Before the "Nice to Do"

There are many bright, shiny security toys, and plenty of vendors are willing to sell them to you. Resist these until you've taken care of the basics. It's fine to let security team members experiment with new stuff as part of their training and development, but your first focus needs to be on requirements, not options.

Identify Important Things

The definition of *important* will change with every company. This is the place where you can add your professional expertise and help determine what the company needs to care about. Consider the following categories to identify the things that matter most to you.

Threats

A review of any number of industry threat intelligence reports can help you identify threats to your type of business. Make sure your functions help address those types of threats (of course, considering impact and likelihood). Nothing will scuttle the relevancy of your program faster than focusing on things that don't really impact your type of business. Plan for what threatens your industry/company.

Consider three kinds of threats:

- Threats that have already impacted your company, such as phishing, ignorant insiders, or ransomware. If the company has experienced an event but has not yet addressed the root cause, this might be a place to add team members to assist.

- Industry threats. What kinds of threats are likely based on your industry, and do you have functions to address them?
- Nation-state threats. You might not be a government, but the cyberwars going on between governments will blow back on your company. What kinds of threats does this introduce, and is your team prepared to respond?

Business Goals

Do the functions your team provides and the structure of your team support your organization's business goals? This can be tricky to discern, particularly in larger organizations that might have many "business goals." Take time to understand the "why" and "what" and then evaluate whether your security priorities support those goals. If your company is very consumer-focused, perhaps you need to provide security services that directly support consumers or support your front-line teams. If the business is cloud-native, making sure your security stack supports cloud-based services is important.

Always show alignment to the business as a prime directive for building your team.

Security Support Functions

As you build out your team, there will be support functions that will be necessary to run the business of security — finance, marketing, metrics/reporting, analytics, and so on. Don't overlook the importance of these functions when you think about building your team. Do you need your own chief of staff? Often, you will be using services from other parts of the organization, but sometimes you need to hire and train nonsecurity people yourself. Regardless of whether support functions are insourced or outsourced, these functions need to be efficient and effective. Make sure you have capable support functions.

If you can find functions that address all these categories (hygiene, compliance, and important things), then that is great. Chase after those things first. Be prepared to pivot, and make sure your team is prepared, too. Things change fast!

Identify Areas of Weakness

Doing a basic strengths and weaknesses analysis is great, but to really understand how the existing security team is working, you need to talk to many people. Start by talking to the security team because they'll likely know where all the good and less-good things are happening. Talk to partners and stakeholders. You'll find out what they think about the effectiveness of the team. Note that I didn't say that you should only talk to "customers" (although they might be stakeholders, too). You must talk to all the people who can influence the team's success or who can have their success influenced by the security function.

Ask some questions to help you understand:

- What do they think the role of security is? Is security a service provider? A strategic partner? Administrative overhead?
- Do they think the team is effective? Do they know what the security team does? Do they think it's done well? What would they like to see done differently?
- Do they think the team is good at partnership and collaboration? Does the security team's work support stakeholders' goals and objectives? Does security support the organizational mission?
- Do they find the security tools and processes effective or disruptive?
- What do they think the security team should be doing differently? What should they be doing more of?

Building a security team isn't only about adding head count. It's about making sure that the entire ecosystem of people, processes, and tools are working together to achieve the organization's mission, as well as the security team's mission. Once you've identified weak areas, you need to decide if you want to discontinue those areas or double down on making those areas strong.

Discontinuing a Function

Sometimes, you need to stop doing something. It could be because the function is solving for a problem that no longer exists. It could be that even though the function was a great idea, it isn't as successful as it needs to be in practice. Perhaps the adoption of the function is less than expected. Perhaps it costs too much compared to the security value you get. Regardless, as the leader, you need to move decisively to make changes when you find those functions.

If you have identified something that is weak — and that your stakeholders think is great — you'll need to be doubly sure to explain your thinking to stakeholders before you take steps to discontinue a function. This is sometimes difficult to do, and it takes time to help them see your perspective. Take time to bring them around. Unilaterally getting rid of something or someone popular can cause distrust with your stakeholders.

If employees are involved (compared to, say, an outsourced function), consider retraining, reskilling, and realigning the people to more needed functions. This can take time but is usually worth the effort. The remaining team can see that there is a willingness to invest in them, which will add to the retention and maintain institutional knowledge. If this is an option, start by talking to the impacted employees early and check in with them often. If they don't want to reskill for another function or don't have the aptitude for performing the new function, check to see if they might fit better in another role elsewhere in the organization. And don't drag out any terminations. Be transparent and be supportive of the team (both the people leaving and the people remaining) as you work through the transition.

Be clear with stakeholders that you're making the change. Let them know that you've heard their comments and are making this change in response to their input. Let them know how the resources will be redeployed and how that will improve the organization's security posture.

Building New Functions

Creating new processes and adding new staff not only help the security posture of the entire organization but also help the rest of the security team learn new things, generally improving the entire security team.

The reality is that in most organizations, security is still seen as administrative overhead. People don't want to spend any more money on it than they absolutely have to. So, before you go asking for more funds, make sure the team you currently have is as efficient as possible. Self-funding by discontinuing ineffective functions and redirecting the resources to the new thing is a great place to start if this is an option. Regardless, make sure you can demonstrate that you're making good stewardship decisions before asking for more.

Creating something new takes time. You cannot do it in half measure. You need to be clear on what it will take to really do this thing well — in terms of people, process, tools, and stakeholder engagement. Be clear on how you will measure the success of the function before you start it!

Getting senior-level buy-in for a new thing is important. It cannot just be the idea of the security team (even if it is). It must be a collective investment in the function. Identify one or two key stakeholders who will champion your function with other people and keep them close throughout the deployment and ongoing operational activities. They will be your best partners if the function causes waves in the organization.

You also can't do new things as a "hobby." It's okay to start with a minimally supported "proof of concept," but if you're going to commit to a new thing, make sure the commitment is appropriate for the target end state. Starting with a minimal "use case" as the basis for the function can be a way to get a foot in the door of doing something new, but this approach can be fraught with problems. Is the use case you've chosen scalable? Does the use case represent the majority of threats/needs you're trying to address, or is it an edge case? Is the group you're partnering with for the use case representative of other partners across the organization, or are they unicorns whose success won't translate anywhere else in the company? Start with your end state in mind and work backward.

If you're in a high-growth organization, you might be able to launch multiple new things simultaneously — congratulations! If not, make sure a new thing is functioning well before moving to the next new thing. Otherwise, you risk burnout and stakeholder frustration, which will damage your ability to do new things in the future.

Building a team is like building a house: start with a strong foundation and intentionally build security "rooms" (functions) on it. That way, if threats change, funding dries up, or a merger/acquisition occurs, you have a security structure that can flex to those changes and still be true to the organization's mission, as well as those of the security team.

What's Next?

- Document your observations and your plan of action to address gaps and opportunities.
- Talk to stakeholders about your observations, and sense-check it with your team and peers.
- Put a planning day on your schedule at least every quarter to do this all over again. Make it part of your cycle of work.
- Update your security strategy to reflect your plan of action timelines and outcomes.

CHAPTER

18

How Do I Write a Job Posting?

Summary

- **Know what you need:** Ask only for what you need a candidate to bring to the role. If you can train on the job, don't make that a required skill.
- **Network:** Use the power of your network to quality check your postings and to amplify them when they get published.
- **Stay curious:** Use apps that check your posting language for bias, check into websites that list common skills and experience criteria for similar jobs.

- **Communicate well and often:** Let everyone know you're hiring and what you're looking for. Make sure your recruiters are posting your jobs in places that will attract a diverse candidate pool.

You're a security leader now, which means that you are running a team and hopefully growing it. At some point, you will need to write a job description with an accompanying job posting. The job posting will be used by recruiters to attract the best and brightest talent. You need to make sure the talent comes on board quickly; there is no time to waste. You need to ensure the posting attracts as much diverse talent as possible to ensure the best possible team. And you need to do all of this without a lot of guidance or previous examples.

My Story

Like most hiring managers, I have never taken a formal class on how to write a job posting. I've written lots of postings, from junior to senior positions, and I still don't feel like I have it right. When I write a job posting, I feel the weight of responsibility to ensure that the posting attracts the best, most diverse talent possible.

I know that the job posting often makes a candidate choose to apply for a job — or not. The job posting is the first thing many candidates know about the company or team — and first impressions count. As a result, I try to cram as much useful information into the posting as possible (usually word limited by the recruiting tools used by my company), and it never seems to be sufficient.

When I was younger, I didn't think at all about what it takes to write a posting; I was too focused on comparing myself to the requirements and finding myself lacking. As I've progressed through my career, job postings have morphed into position descriptions. (I know they're not supposed to be the same thing as a posting, but often they are!) I am still frustrated that I'm not describing the position well enough for candidates. I don't know if my perception of job postings results from how they are constructed or how they are used. I just know that in my experience, job postings are a barrier to a new job, not a tool to open doors to new opportunities.

When I write a job description, I try to put myself in the position of the candidate. Is the role clear? Are the skills I'm asking for really necessary, or will I train them on the job? Does a candidate know how the role fits into and supports the company? Can anyone see themselves in this role? Instead of making the posting a hurdle that the applicant must overcome, I try to make it an invitation to a relationship.

As for my own candidacy, I've now reached a place in my career where people ask me to write my own position description. (I still respond to traditional job postings, too.) Telling an employer what you want to do is easier said than done! It's great to be in such a position, but it can be harder than responding to a posting someone else wrote. How risky is it to write your own job description? If you forget to add something, you have no one to blame but yourself! If you fail at your job, what does that mean when you created the position? What if you write a new job for yourself and then you find out later that you don't like the job?

The Challenge of Job Postings

The security industry argues among itself. Is it that there isn't enough talent, or are we asking for the wrong things? Is it that the talent just doesn't exist, or are we looking in the wrong place? There is only one thing to do. We need to make sure we are creating job postings that are as good as possible, and we need to circulate them in as many places as possible. We need to be as expansive and welcoming as we can be.

So why is this so hard? It is because security people write bad job postings.

Have you read any job postings lately? They're easy to find. Just go to any job board and look for information security or cybersecurity jobs. (There is no consistency in the labels we give security jobs.) Take a look at the way the job is described. Does the posting show how the role fits into the organization, why it's needed, and who it supports? Does the posting require an appropriate type of background and experience, or is it looking for a unicorn blend of history and talent that is impossible to find? Does the posting clearly articulate what to expect in the hiring process, who the hiring manager is (or at least what position that person holds), and other important logistics? I'm guessing that you'll find some of these things in some of the postings and that no posting will have everything it needs.

Few security professionals have been trained on how to write a job posting, and it shows. Before you publish that job position, make sure you get a second or third opinion from peers, staff, and HR partners. Use applications that assess your language for bias. Writing job postings is not a core skill, so get help from people who do this professionally. In the meantime, if you're creating job postings for your own team, consider the things discussed in the following sections.

Skills

Of all the challenges with security job postings, the skills mismatch causes most candidates to skip your posting and look elsewhere. The industry has a skills gap, yet our job postings require too many skills and too many certifications. Also, there is an assumption that the successful candidate must arrive in the new job fully trained to do whatever is needed. Before you sit down to write your posting, fully consider the skills that are absolutely required from a new hire, as well as the skills you are willing to help the candidate develop on the job.

When you are considering skills, you should also consider what formal education you expect in your candidates. Don't ask for a four-year degree unless you truly believe it's a necessary requirement. (Most security leaders do not.) Be careful about the certifications you require; do they really support the role you are hiring for? Are there equivalences you are willing to consider, such as work experience in place of formal schooling? Must all the training you require be security-specific, or can you let candidates demonstrate skills through another path? How do you feel about self-taught candidates?

Benchmark yourself against other postings and resources, such as the U.S. National Initiative for Cybersecurity Education (NICE) Workforce framework. Make sure you're not asking a junior candidate to have senior-level skills. Make sure the senior-level job posting isn't asking for too much experience or technology mastery. Just because it is a senior position doesn't mean the role requires expert-level mastery of every skill!

Differentiate between general IT skills (such as programming languages) and security skills (assessing applications for insecure code), and make sure you're not labeling a job "security" just because it sits in the security organization. It's perfectly fine for a CISO to hire a generic application developer, project manager, or data analyst without making them a "security engineer," "security manager," or "security analyst."

Interestingly, when you talk to hiring managers, it is often *not* the technical skills that are hard to develop on the job — it's the professional skills like empathy, teamwork, and communication. When you read the job description, which "required skills" are listed first? The technical skills! If you think you can train the technical skills on the job but want to hire the professional skills, list the professional skills first.

Don't ask for skills or experience you are willing to live without. Even putting unnecessary skills in the "optional" or "preferred" section is enough to turn high-quality candidates away — so make sure the skills you put into your job postings are ones you truly require.

Context

No job is created in isolation. If you're hiring someone into a role, it is because your organization needs that role for some purpose, and that purpose aligns with your security strategy and the organizational business goals and mission.

So, when you're creating a job posting, let potential candidates know the "why" of the job. Why does this job exist? What purpose does it fill? How does it fit into the company, the security team, the security function? Is the role focused on one single line of business in the company or the whole company? Is the role going to be part of a revenue-generating team or a product support team, or will it be an administrative function? What are your core values, and how does this position support them? Include a link to the important parts of your company website so a candidate can quickly see general information about working at your company.

Don't just talk about what the job is; talk about how the company will support the development of the candidate. Tell the candidate what they become, as well as what the job can become. Do you invest in training employees on the job, send them to conferences, or pay for industry memberships? Then say so! Let them know that you will be helping them grow when they join your team, not just assessing their job performance. Let them know that the risk they are taking to apply for your job is worth it.

You should give candidates some context because it allows them to see themselves in the role. Candidates want to be excited about a new opportunity. If all you can do is tell them that they will be monitoring vulnerabilities, pentesting an application, or writing policy, you're not giving them the full picture.

> Giving candidates the "why" allows them to fill out the role in their imagination and allows them to imagine their success as part of your team.

Context will allow candidates to be better prepared for interviews, ask better questions, and be better prepared to do what you need.

Language

When you're creating a job posting, you are creating a vision for the candidate. You're telling a story of what the role can be and what their role in it will look like. So, just like any good storyteller, you need to put the reader in the center of the story — not as a passive observer, but as the whole point. To do this, you need to use the first-person language.

Instead of saying, "The candidate will monitor systems and follow playbooks to respond to incidents," you might choose to say, "You will use your powers of observation to identify anomalies and attacks against your company."

Instead of saying, "Applicants will be part of the Security team," you might say, "You will be a key member of a highly professional and inclusive group of people who ensure the security of the entire company."

When you write your job postings, you should be careful to avoid language that is seen as gendered, biased, or otherwise promotes negative stereotypes. Some people want to be "rock stars," but for others, this is seen as a masculine, high-competition standard that automatically excludes women or other minorities. There is free software available to check the language you plan to use. Search for "bias language applications" to see some options. Please use them. Candidates will *not* apply for your job if the language you use prevents them from seeing themselves as being successful in the role.

If you can, try to avoid using filter Q&A as the first step in the application process. Companies love to do this — it helps their algorithms "weed out" unqualified candidates. But security jobs aren't cookie-cutter, and these algorithms often do more harm than good because they filter out qualified candidates who lack exactly the right kind of experience or use the wrong words in their résumés. Our algorithms aren't ready for the lack of structure currently existing in the security profession. If you *must* use these, ask your recruiter to see the reject list as well as the selection list. You'll be surprised who gets left behind!

Where You Post

If you are looking for the biggest possible pool of talent, it is important to consider where you post and what you post. Be explicit with your recruiter (if you have one) to understand where they post, and push them to think about security-specific and nontraditional posting locations.

Big-name posting boards are a great place to start to get wide coverage of traditional candidates. They are great in terms of volume and reach. This is typically where company recruiters will start and end. The title and tags of your job posting can be super important; security jobs can get lost in the volume. For example, a candidate searching for "security" jobs can drown in a sea of physical security positions, completely irrelevant. Alternatively, a candidate searching for "cybersecurity" positions might miss your "information security" posting.

Professional security organizations (ISACA, ISC2, ISSA, and so on) are good places to find existing security talent, although you might need to take out membership to use their job boards. Candidates are already engaged in the security community, so these postings are good if you're looking for a mid- to upper-level candidate. Entry-level candidates might not have found these boards yet, so don't spend time posting entry-level roles in these places.

Don't overlook the role of social media in amplifying your postings. If you maintain an active LinkedIn, Twitter, or other social media presence, you can push your open positions through these channels. Using hashtags to engage minority groups works really well here, too. Ask your team to use their own accounts to get the word out. Many minority groups will give preference to posts from trusted colleagues, rather than cold posting to a generic job board. Use your network and your team's network to get the word out to underrepresented communities.

What's Next?

Some hiring managers use their job postings as a bar that needs to be cleared in order to get the "best talent." I argue that the job posting should be the *minimum* standard you need for a person in the role, not the maximum. The posting needs to be welcoming and non-prescriptive to allow as many people as possible to see themselves as a good fit for your role.

- Practice by writing a job posting for your job. How would you make the language inclusive? What skills do you *really* need? What did you learn on the job? Compare this to the job description that was used when you applied for the position. What is different? Why? (By the way, this is a great exercise for anyone on your team who has hiring responsibility.)
- Take some of your existing job postings and run them through the antibias language applications. What words need to be changed?
- Talk to your recruiters to understand their process from beginning to end. Where do they post jobs? How long do posts stay active? How do they market open jobs? Where can you add to this so that your jobs go to as many communities as possible?
- Check out the NICE framework (https://www.nist.gov/itl/applied-cybersecurity/nice/nice-framework-resource-center) and Cyberseek.org for U.S.-based resources on skills, salaries, and other benchmarking items.
- Investigate diversity and inclusion in cybersecurity networking groups for their hashtags to use in your postings.

CHAPTER

19

How Do I Encourage Diversity?

Summary

- **Know yourself:** Know what you want to focus on and set metrics to measure your progress.
- **Network:** Get to know diversity networking groups. Learn from them and partner with them to improve your workplace and your job postings.
- **Stay curious:** Listen to all your employees to ensure they feel included, respected, and supported. Find regular ways to solicit feedback from your entire team.
- **Communicate well and often:** Let everyone know this is an issue you care about and share what you learn.

- **Know talent:** Truly learn how to spot, assess, and develop talent. Then trust this skill when you observe or experience the exceptional, especially when they don't talk, look, or act as you expect.
- **Mentor:** You will find your "diamonds in the rough" in places where you won't expect. They will be unpolished, diverse or not. Learn how to help your team unlock the best of themselves and believe in themselves — especially diverse talent!

Building the community you want and need is one of the fun parts of being a security leader. However, questions of diversity might not come up when you first start out. Instead, managers reach a point in their careers (and in their maturity as managers) when they start to pay attention to equity issues. This mostly occurs when someone has been a manager for a while and has largely mastered basic management skills.

When this happens, a leader must start with what they have. The manager leads a small team with low turnover or a fast-growing team. Either way, there are ways to intentionally foster a diverse team of people with different styles, backgrounds, and experiences who will contribute to the higher performance of the team.

> By any measurement, security is not an industry known for its diversity. Therefore, managers will need to pay particular attention in order to develop a diverse team.

Proportionally, security has fewer women, fewer black and brown people, and fewer LGBTQ+ people than other technology and science, technology, engineering, and math (STEM) professions. It doesn't have to be this way, and there are many initiatives underway within companies and the industry to address the gap. Security teams struggle with our collective image. If we see minority people, they're often in a sales or human resources (HR) or support an adjacent role. We don't see minority people as often in the core technology, security, or risk functions. Find those people; get to know them, build relationships, and seek their help to achieve your goals and make your team better.

Considering diversity and how to foster inclusivity and equity in your team is an ongoing learning activity. People are not their labels, and many people have multiple diversity attributes simultaneously. As a manager, it can be overwhelming to learn how to manage this all at once. The point is to begin doing it and to stay open to learning new things. It is an opportunity to help ourselves and make our own lives better.

Start with Numbers

Diversity has many meanings to many people. Start by understanding what it means to you and your company. Are you interested in bringing in any level of underrepresented people, or do you have a target in mind? If so, what is that target, and why that number? Are you close to it or far away? Maybe your goal isn't a fixed number; instead, maybe you want to move closer to something different than you have now, so what would that look like?

It's reasonable to consider the representative population for your current location (as small as a town or as large as a nation). What proportion of the population is male, female, or other? What percentage is black or brown? What percentage are immigrants or first-generation nationalities? LGBTQ+? What are the age demographics for the area? Think about the location of your hiring pool, and then think about your current team. Do they equitably represent the community in which they work?

Matching your team to the community proportions does not have to be your end goal, but it is a place to begin.

Another approach popular in the technology industry is to look to your customers. Are they diverse? Sentiment analysis can measure how well your current team is meeting the needs of your customers from a variety of backgrounds. Many teams then use this data to aim for team member representation that closely resembles their customer or partner base. Beyond seizing the diversity dividend, this approach can also enable your teams to better serve and support customers, your nontechnology partners, and the business.

Create your base numbers, and then see where you have opportunities. Look to keep the diverse talent you already have and add to it as your team grows or as employee turnover occurs. Over time, you can move the needle.

Understand Your Cultural Issues

It is no good running out to hire diverse talent if those people can't be successful, supported, and celebrated in your organization once they arrive. Consider how your team operates and their environment, and ask yourself and others whether your environment supports diverse staff.

Start with the physical environment. What artwork is on the walls of your office? What images are used in your presentation materials? Are there spaces that support breastfeeding? Are there quiet spaces for introverts, as well as group spaces for extroverted collaboration? When the team has a shared meal, are ethnic foods included on the menu? Is your space wheelchair-, service dog-, or neurodiverse-friendly? These often-forgotten details can have a significant impact on creating an environment where your diverse team can thrive. A quick anecdote adds to this importance: A fellow leader once told a story of always seeing one of his brightest team members in the restroom with a backpack, sometimes three or four times a day. One day, he kindly inquired about what the man was doing and learned that the man was Muslim and was praying on a rug in a toilet stall because there were no prayer rooms. Needless to say, a prayer room was available the next day for all to use. The point is that if winning matters, building diverse teams matters and so does getting these details right.

What pronouns do you use when you're talking to your team or about people in general? What commonly used technical language has historical roots in bias? Representation (or lack of it) matters and is noticed. Find alternatives to referring to groups of people as *you guys*. Consider using *block lists* or *allow lists* instead of *blacklists* (deny-lists) or *white lists* (allow-lists). Stop defaulting to using pronouns such as *he and him* (or worse, using *him* for everything except assistants who are her). Consider using *they*, *them*, and *their* instead. As the leader, you model the behavior you want, and your leadership in these areas will shape your entire organization.

Understand your existing staff. Are there people on the team, particularly managers, who are known to make insensitive remarks? Or worse, are they known to do something that is illegal or invokes harassment? Are your leaders creating psychologically safe environments for women and diverse talent? Make sure your entire team has access to training and awareness materials around diversity, equity, and inclusion (DEI) issues, and be clear on your expectations for their behavior. Equally important, take an active role in setting the tone for what is acceptable and what isn't. Tell your leaders and teams what you will or won't stand for. Set the red line and hold your leaders and teams responsible for building and sustaining the culture you want. Diversity problems are often culture problems in hiding.

Do some research on how to make an inclusive work environment and see where you stack up. You might need to have conversations with your own management chain, HR support, or others — but begin at the beginning. Talk about the issue with your team and other work colleagues. Be a vocal supporter of diversity groups and issues. Get your house in order before you ask someone to come into it.

There are lots of great resources — written and in-person — to learn from. Most companies are continuing to experiment to see what works. Keep learning!

Attracting Diverse Talent

Diverse talent is out there. I repeat: diverse talent is out there. For some managers, it is difficult to know where to go to find it. Answer? Networking. As a leader, you need to get out into the community and make it known that you welcome diverse employees and team members. (This isn't just about hiring into your own team; it also means advocating for diversity in all the teams across your company.) Engage with groups Women in Cybersecurity (WiCys.org) or the International Consortium of Minority Cybersecurity Professionals (ICMCP.org) to understand what employees need to be treated equitably and to build recruiting partnerships.

Have a social media presence (Twitter, LinkedIn, Instagram, and so on) and tag diversity groups when your company is posting an open position. Social media can help you have a presence in places you don't typically go, and if you create a reputation for caring about diversity and inclusion, word will spread. (If you *don't* care about it, that will spread, too.)

The following are some diversity hashtags you can use on social media:

- @wisporg
- #ShareTheMicInCyber
- @ICMCP_ORG
- @WiCySorg
- #BlackTechTwitter
- #infosecjobs
- #Neurodiversity
- #Womenintech
- #WomenInCyber
- #veteransemployment

Don't be shy about personally inviting diverse candidates to apply for your positions. Particularly in security, underrepresented groups are well-connected and know when a manager or organization will support their careers. Make yourself known to these groups, and you will open previously overlooked doors. Find ways to speak with employee networking groups and industry groups about this issue. Listen to what diverse groups tell you about what they need and how you can help.

Consider establishing relationships with "feeder" organizations that can be a talent pipeline. Perhaps there is a local community college or university with diverse students. Perhaps there are online boot camps that target veterans, foster kids, or women, and perhaps you can sponsor a student (or a program)! Consider national (Pers Scholars, for example) or regional apprenticeship programs. Invest in building sustainable pipelines for overlooked talent, and you will tap into a literal goldmine that can transform your team. Mentor underrepresented people. They will learn a ton from you, and I guarantee you will learn a ton from them. They will also amplify any positions you have available — and maybe even apply themselves.

Writing the Job Description and Posting

One of the biggest barriers to attracting a diverse candidate pool is the typical job advertisement. The point of a job posting is to allow a candidate to see themselves in the role — not to filter out arbitrarily unsuitable candidates. Your definition of "unsuitable" will be based on your own experiences and biases, so let diverse candidates open your eyes to ways of thinking about skills, background, and experience that you might not have considered.

Again, do some research on how to write a job description that will allow diverse candidates to consider applying. In short, require only the things you *absolutely* require — nothing more. If you can, get rid of the "preferred skills" section — either you need a skill or you don't. Take time to explain how this position fits your team and how your team fits in the company. (See Chapter 18, "How Do I Write a Job Posting?" for more details.)

Emphasize how the organization will support a candidate's development through training, work and life balance, championship, mentorship, sponsorship, and so on. No one will satisfy every requirement right from the start. (If they do, why would they want your job? They already know everything.) Diverse candidates pay more attention to cultural fit and working conditions than more traditional candidates — because diverse candidates must work harder, and they have more to lose when the fit isn't good. So make sure they know, right from the start, what to expect if they join you and your team.

If you post a position and your candidate pool lacks candidates with diverse backgrounds, consider rewriting and reposting it. Ask yourself (and others) what might need to be changed in the way it was written or advertised to attract a diverse candidate slate. Leverage your networks and social media to ask for constructive feedback from diverse people across the varied spectrums — neurodiverse, veterans, underrepresented minorities, LGBTQ+, and others. Don't be shy about trying again.

The Interviewing Process

So, you have a diverse candidate pool, and you now need to select a candidate. Again, research how to structure your selection process to be as bias-free as possible. (There are a *ton* of resources out there to help you with this.)

Consider "blind" selection processes. If it's not already part of your HR process, you can facilitate this within your own team. One way is to get all the candidate résumés, remove the names/addresses, and share them with the selection panel. (Make sure there is more than one person making filtering decisions.) Help your selection committee overcome their own biases as much as possible.

Have a group of people be part of the interview process, and make the group appropriate for the level of the role. (A candidate for a junior position doesn't need to meet with 25 people or the chief executive of the company!) This team can help the hiring manager select from the pool of candidates, interview the selected candidates, and recommend a final hiring decision to the manager. Make sure the team knows what the role is, what kind of skills/experience you want your candidate to have, and how to assess the candidates. If a nondiverse interviewing team interviews your candidates, you will be less likely to appeal to diverse applicants. (Don't forget, an interview is a two-way street. They are interviewing you just as much as you are interviewing them.) Make sure the people who engage with the applicants are as diverse as possible. Bring in people from outside your immediate team, if necessary. (This is probably necessary if your team is homogeneous.)

There has been a technology trend to "test" candidates' subject-matter knowledge during the interview process. This is controversial for any candidate, but it is particularly controversial for diverse candidates. If you decide you must have a test as part of the hiring process, make this clear from the beginning, and do what you can to make the test as bias-free as possible. In fact, make the entire hiring process clear from the start. Let potential candidates know what is involved, so they can judge whether the process is worth their time. How many interviews? Is there a test? Do they have to give a presentation or submit a paper as part of the process? When do you plan to hire? This will help with your diverse candidates, as well as with all candidates.

Retaining Diverse Talent

You have hired a person from an underrepresented group. Great work! How do you make sure your lack of inclusive practices isn't a reason they would choose to leave your organization? Even more, how do you retain this talent for as long as it is valuable to you both?

Make sure all managers have training on managing diverse teams and that they have received inherent bias training. People join companies, but they leave managers, so if you and other managers don't have the training/skills to support diversity, you and they need to learn. This training should happen before the hiring begins, but in reality, this is a skill that managers should be retrained on and be regularly held accountable to.

Provide employee networking support. Here are some challenging questions for most leaders: Do you know all your diverse talent? If they saw you in the hallway, would you recognize them by name, story, or accomplishment? Or do you only get to know diverse talent when it comes to recruiting and retaining? It is possible that you (and your leadership) do not know your diverse talent. What's more, it's possible that your diverse talent doesn't know each other. If your company is large enough, create employee networking groups, such as "women in tech," "minorities in security," "working parents," "LGBTQ+ alliances," and so on. Make sure you and other managers are actively part of those groups as well. If your company isn't large enough to have your own networking groups, find groups in your area (or online) and encourage your employees (all of them, not just the minorities) to participate. Bonus if you and your managers attend as well, regardless of their own diversity characteristics.

As you check in with your employees, make sure you're asking each of them how they are feeling about working on your team. Do they feel supported? Included? Valued? Regardless of their minority status, we need to ensure all our teams are motivated to continue being part of the team. For minority employees, this is even more important — but don't ask *only* them. Ask every member of your team — often. How are they feeling? What's working? What's not working? What could be better? Keeping tabs on the feelings of your team will help every member of your team — and you. Don't wait for an annual employee survey to give you these answers. Ask these questions frequently so that it normalizes the asking.

Promotions and Career Development

Like all employees, underrepresented people need to know they are being invested in, that there are opportunities for growth, and that they are equally represented in leadership. It's not helpful to bring people into the organization only to have them leave when they hit the ceiling or are pigeonholed.

Provide opportunities for visibility and growth. Review who is being offered key projects, and make sure your diverse employees are considered for these roles. Make sure your diverse employees aren't only being considered for supporting roles. They need to be exposed to leadership skills and opportunities, too. Make sure they are being given opportunities to stretch and to perhaps fail — safely. Sponsorship matters, especially among diverse talent. If you or your organization is not sponsoring and championing growth, your diverse talent will leave your organization for one that will.

Recognize good work across your whole team, not just the "star players." A successful team is, well, a *team*, so recognizing only some of the team misses the point. No one achieves good work on their own, so recognize the whole team contribution.

When it's time to do a performance review or make a promotion, take a step back and look at the big picture. Who's being put forward as a top performer? Who is not doing well? Start with the individual facts but then compare across the group. Are there others who are being unfavorably and unfairly compared? Are you holding some people to a higher (or lower) standard than others? It helps to look at group trends to make sure people are being considered appropriately for their contributions to their team.

Make sure managers are providing feedback to their employees that is practical and timely. Ensure managers aren't shying away from difficult conversations with any employees, particularly minority employees. Again, manager training on how to provide appropriate coaching and feedback is essential.

Leaving the Team

When any employee leaves your team for a new role or leaves the company altogether, make sure you do an exit interview, and make sure that the interview investigates the culture of the team. Find out what is working and what isn't. As a manager/leader, you might not want to be the person who does the interview. This is where HR or an independent person can really help. However the exit interview is conducted, find a way to get honest and unvarnished feedback about how employees feel in your organization, and make sure you act on the feedback!

The truth is you will not change the makeup of your team overnight. To make change, you need to be intentional, and you need to be in it for the long haul. Your leadership words and actions are the most important element for building a diverse team. You must walk the walk every day, and the rest of the organization needs to do the same. It isn't easy, and you will need to be prepared for stumbles because you will stumble! Being sincere and authentic will help you out — a lot! Alternatively, if you're insincere about caring for people, it is immediately apparent to everyone around you. Building a diverse team will happen only if you sincerely care about all the individuals on your team, support their personal growth, and encourage their whole selves at work. This takes time and effort, but doing so is worth it.

What's Next?

- Evaluate your work location and create a baseline before you begin any specific diversity actions.
- Take time to consider your workplace. Is it designed to support minority employees?

- Learn about employee or community network groups for minorities — bonus if they are focused on security. Know how to contact them for job postings and networking opportunities.
- Consider your promotion process. What checks and balances exist in the process to ensure that minority candidates are being equitably reviewed and promoted?

CHAPTER

20

How Do I Manage Up?

Summary

- **Know your manager:** Explicitly ask how they like to communicate. How often? What channels? Verbal or written?
- **Educate:** Make sure you are personally growing the security acumen of senior leadership. The more they learn from you, the easier it will be to work with them.
- **Establish your authority:** Take every leadership interaction as an opportunity to demonstrate your competency and leadership. This will help them trust you to make the right decisions.
- **Communicate well and often:** Report regularly to senior management about the security program, external security events and trends, and your role within it.

Being a security leader is about more than simply managing a security program. A successful leader manages their management chain and senior stakeholders. This part of the job is as important, if not more so, than running the security tools and services that make up the security function. Why is this so important?

Most security leaders report to someone who doesn't understand security. Even a chief information officer (CIO) boss, who you would think might be most likely to understand, doesn't spend their time in the weeds of information risk management, which means they often fail to consider the nuances of security strategy and decision-making. Many security leaders report to a nontechnical executive — a financial officer, the head of the legal department, or even the chief executive officer (CEO) — and those people rarely have any security background either. Even though they are ultimately the decision-makers and overseers of the security program (in publicly traded companies), board members rarely have anyone with an understanding of security.

As a security leader, you must work with your management chain daily to ensure the security program is funded, supported, and maintained. You also need to work with them during a security incident when tensions are high and time is short. Managing up is a critical skill for both of these tasks. Unfortunately, it is one that new and experienced security leaders struggle with. Most of us received no skills training for influencing up and are learning on the job. Before you even start your new job, make sure you identify your leaders and have a plan for partnership and engagement.

Who Are Senior Stakeholders?

Your senior stakeholder and the number of layers of management you need to manage will be determined by the size and structure of your organization. The stakeholders listed in the following sections are the most common.

Your Immediate Manager

As always, your immediate manager is the first person you need to make sure is well-managed. In his book *The First 90 Days*, Michael D. Watkins discusses how to begin on the right foot with your manager by having a series of conversations that uncover how to work together. It is important to discuss questions of expectations, style, and so on early.

Also, the security leader must have early conversations with their manager to understand how they think about security, risk, and compliance. The following are some things you need to learn:

- How do they perceive the security function? Do they think security is a business enabler, an administrative burden, or something else?
- How do they assess risk? Do they need evidence of an active event before they act, or are they willing to pre-invest in security controls? Do they have their own risk concerns they are worried about now, or will they leave it to you to tell them what they should be concerned about?
- How much autonomy will you have? Do you need to run everything by and through them, or can you make business cases to other stakeholders without significant input from your manager?
- How well do they understand security terminology? Can they stay with you as you discuss kill chains, zero trust, or the MITRE ATT&CK Framework? Or are they still trying to work out how to recognize vulnerabilities?

It is important to understand how savvy your boss is regarding security topics and how engaged they want to be in security decision-making. There are no right or wrong answers to these questions. Answers are just information to be considered as you think about what your manager is going to need from you — and you from them — to be successful.

Senior Leaders

As the security leader — and regardless of your place in the organization — you will need to engage senior leaders in all disciplines to help them understand how security will impact their worlds and how they will impact yours.

Obviously, some roles are more impactful to the security program than others, such as financial officers who can give you funding, legal officers who can help with compliance and regulations, and IT leaders who set technology strategies. Less-obvious senior roles will need to be nurtured, such as communications leaders who will help sell your services internally and externally, human resources directors who will enable employee processes, and business leaders who will decide how security is positioned within their units.

Within the IT organization, there are plenty of people in leadership positions who can make or break your security program. Most security leaders report through the CIO. (Although that's changing, and in smaller organizations, the CIO and the chief information security officer might be the same person.) You will need to pay close attention to these relationships. Anyone who is leading technology architecture will be a primary partner. The head of application development or management will need to be kept close. Systems administration director? Networking? Yes, they all count. You might need to delegate some of this relationship-building to your own direct reports. It's hard to be in so many places at once, but based on the technology strategies and priorities of your organization, you must build relationships with these leaders.

The challenge is that there can be many people in leadership positions, and there's only one of you. And these leaders will have different priorities that you have. Knowing what they care about is your first task. Aligning your security program to address security while also incorporating their priorities is a close second. Maximizing your influence on the group is an important consideration. Decide who will receive targeted attention and who will receive general attention. Then you need to work with each accordingly.

Board Members

All security leaders — in private or public sectors — will have a governance group that sits outside the organization's day-to-day management. This group oversees the security function as part of the overall management of the organization. For simplicity's sake, I will refer to them as *board members*. If this group is functioning effectively, they will not be involved in operational decisions; instead, they will want to know if the organization is appropriately managing the information and technology risks.

A security leader will need to work with other senior leaders to tell the right story to manage this relationship. Each organization will do this differently, so the security leader must defer to the internal processes to create and present the story. Board members need to know the following:

- How is the security program organized? (For example, what frameworks and organizing structures are in place?)
- Who is responsible for the security program? Not just the security leader, but what business leader is ultimately accountable for the program's success?
- What are the current and likely threats that must be managed? This will depend on the industry sector, location, and other factors.

- How well is the program performing? Some of the answers will be data/metrics-driven; some will be qualitative.
- How does the organization compare to others? Benchmarking might be included in the previous question, but here, the board is really asking, "Are we doing enough?"

More than anything else, board members need to have confidence that the security leader is capable and honest.

Regardless of how often you present to the board, take every opportunity to reinforce the perspective that you are a competent security leader. Take advantage of current events to educate them on how your organization is impacted by or defends against a threat. If possible, find ways to have less-formal, off-cycle meetings with committee chairs to give them a deeper understanding of your program and progress. Don't be afraid to talk about what is working and what is not working in the program. Ask them for specific items to help with your program (funding, time, industry leverage, and so on).

Regulators expect board members to be educated about cyber and information security risks, so you can expect them to learn more about this over time. This can be a double-edged sword. They will know enough to understand the terminology but perhaps not enough to understand how it applies to your specific company. Work with them on their journeys to become more proficient because it will serve the company's security program.

Help Them Understand Security

Managing up requires that you and your leadership be communicating effectively. This can happen only if they have the requisite level of security knowledge. Unfortunately, many senior-level managers don't, so one of your first tasks is implementing a plan to help them learn. Your plan should consider formal and informal ways to help bring them up to speed with regular contact regarding security topics. Consider the ideas in the following sections.

Regular Meetings

When you have one-on-one meetings with your manager or senior stakeholders, make sure those meetings are not just about tactical issues of the day. Take the time to share information about topics that will help them learn about security. This can be done in a nonthreatening and emotionally low-key way. It's better to talk about these things when nothing is on fire than trying to educate them during a crisis.

Talk to them about current issues they might be hearing about from the media, such as ransomware, phishing, and breaches in similar companies. Let them know what kinds of issues impact your industry and how your strategic plan activities address those things.

Help them to see what you see in terms of threats and events at the company. Then, talk about what you're doing to address those threats or what you need to address the threats. It doesn't have to result in a request; it's simply to let them know what you're thinking about and what they should be thinking about.

Give them your candid assessment of the strengths and opportunities in your own company. Is the security culture strong? Does your program have support from all parts of the organization? Let them know what you think about the current state of security in the company, and let them stew on what they can do to enable your programs.

Incident Preparation

Preparing your leadership team for a security incident is one of the first things you should do with them. This includes your immediate manager, senior leaders, and the board.

If there is no security incident response plan, you'll need to create one. Ideally, you won't need to create one from scratch. Perhaps there is a basic, non-cybersecurity crisis plan for you to follow. Or maybe the communications group has its own communications hierarchy that can be emulated for creating a cybersecurity plan. Creating an incident response plan is a great way to engage partners and build community. Take advantage of the opportunity to build supporters.

As soon as you have the incident response plan created, it's time to talk to your management chain about their role. This can be a simple meeting to go over the general steps and process flows. This type of meeting is also great to use for any new executives who join the company after you have arrived. You're helping them to be prepared in case an incident occurs. This also sets you up as the person they will engage whenever they have a security question or concern.

Tabletop Exercises

Creating and leading tabletop exercises (TTX) are great ways for you to help your management chain and leadership understand security. You can engage a third party to help you run the TTX or do it yourself. With good TTX, you can introduce security concepts that touch on ideas such as risk management, communication strategies, and chain of command. You can help them understand that security incidents can occur over days and months and that they will need to be prepared for extended incident engagements. You can incorporate regulations, external media inquiries, and multicausal events.

Tabletop exercises are an excellent way for security leaders to learn how your senior leaders think and act under pressure. You will learn what they care most about (such as customers, employees, the supply chain, or something else). You will learn to whom they defer when running a crisis and who takes a back seat. You will learn who is willing to decide and act, even if there isn't much data to support a decision. This knowledge is invaluable as you think about how to structure your security communications and processes.

Participants will get to see you model appropriate crisis-response behavior. This is an opportunity to demonstrate your leadership capabilities, particularly how well you understand the security environment and lead them during a cybersecurity crisis event. Make clear that you *will* be the executive leader in this situation — not the normal crisis management or IT operations crisis teams. You are the owner of the incident process. Use a TTX to show what that means.

Current Events

One of the best ways to "manage up" to your immediate manager, senior leaders, or the board is to find a way to keep them informed of current security events. Some security leaders do this daily by providing a daily incident report that discusses internal and external activities. Some do this monthly. Some do it when there is a newsworthy external event. You will know what your company will tolerate, and I recommend that you give them as much information as you and they can manage.

One idea is to take an external event and give them your inside view of it. Gathering and presenting this information can also be used for quarterly and annual reporting — within the company and with the board. You can cover the following on a single page:

- The details of the event: the what, who, how, when, and why
- Whether the same kind of event could happen to your company and why

- Whether this has occurred in your company before or whether it is currently happening
- The likely impact if it was to happen to your company, in terms of incident response, business impact, and so on
- What is in place to prevent, detect, and respond to this type of incident

Senior leaders want to know that you can be trusted to manage security risks and incidents. Training them on the kind of security events you are watching will help them learn about your leadership and inspire confidence that you are supporting the company.

When Things Go Wrong

Sometime during your tenure, there will likely be a security event that gets the attention of your company's senior leaders. There is no better time to educate them on how security should operate and how you will guide the organization.

When you have an incident, you want to be seen as calm, responsive, and capable. This starts by following the incident response playbook that you have already shared with senior leaders. Be as predictable as possible.

Inevitably, there will be some detail that will not fit neatly into the playbook. When this happens, tell your leadership how you are handling that issue or ask for input and adjust accordingly.

If something negative happens as a result of your leadership or your team, be accountable by acknowledging and addressing the issue. Continue working the playbook.

After the event has concluded, make sure you have a "lessons learned" review that involves the company's senior leaders.

Make them aware of any post-event actions that need to be taken and keep them informed until the work is completed.

Throughout the entire event, make sure you are connected to them and that you are available whenever they need to reach you. For a multiday event, this can also mean letting them know who is covering for you while you rest and recharge and getting back to them as soon as you can.

Managing up through the ranks of leadership is a key skill for all security leaders to acquire. You can incorporate elements of security knowledge into regular meetings or take advantage of current events to become vehicles for learning. Either way, the objective is to put security in front of senior leaders as often as possible in a way that reinforces your professionalism and capabilities. Regular reinforcement will allow you to lean on your ongoing relationships when you must introduce a business case for new funding, make a difficult policy decision, or otherwise need their goodwill.

What's Next?

- Make sure all senior leaders understand your incident response processes and playbooks.
- Identify the senior leaders who need special one-on-one relationship attention.
- Learn how to engage with the board and who needs to be involved in material/presentation preparation.
- Talk to your immediate manager about their understanding of security and risk. Then, if needed, make a plan to help bring their knowledge up to standard.

CHAPTER

21

How Do I Fund My Program?

Summary

- **Know your numbers:** Know your income sources, your spending needs, and how financial decisions are made at your organization.
- **Network:** Know who makes spending decisions and keep regular contact with them about your planning needs.
- **Communicate well and often:** Ask for everything you need, even if you know the answer will be "no." Give them a choice to make and document their risk management choices.

When you are a mid-level security manager, you don't need to care too much about where the money to pay for your programs came from — it sort of magically appears (or not). It is the job of your manager and their manager to get the budget you need. This is a common experience for most of us. (We're happily going along being a manager of people, but income sources are not something we particularly worry about.)

When you become a security leader, suddenly it is your job to ensure there is funding for the team. You must learn how the whole financing thing works. Who makes decisions, officially or unofficially, about how money is spent? What is the budget cycle? When can you ask for money? Even if everyone agrees that security should be invested in, where will the money come from and when?

It can take a lot of time to understand how money works, who should decide where the money should be spent, and how to engage with the institution to ensure that money flows to the security team. Being the security team leader means you must know how much money you need and for what, how you bring value to the organization, and how to tap into funding sources. Although you can learn basic organizational finance in a business class or a book, *how* to make it happen depends on where you work, so be prepared to invest time in learning how this works where you are.

Like me, you might pride yourself in being a pragmatic security leader. You might take pride in pushing an organization just enough to make a security difference but not so much that the organization starts to push back. This is great for rolling out new security tools or services, but if you're leading a security organization, you are not just managing operations; you're managing risk. It took me a while to understand this.

> You must ask for everything you need, knowing that leadership can (and probably will) say "no."

You must force management to understand all that is needed to fund a security program, even if you know the funding isn't available. Saying "no" is a risk decision, and it's management's way of articulating where they are willing to invest their resources. If you don't ask for what you need, they won't know what you need. Sticker shock is real, so don't spring all this on them in one sitting. However, you have an obligation to make them fully aware of everything you need to lead the security program. Don't hide it from them; doing so will only make it harder for you to do your job.

Funding a Team

Most of us start our leadership journeys by running a small team that is focused on a single service area. This is a great place to start understanding how the organization funds and values your team's work.

Start by understanding how your team is funded. Is the cost of your function regarded as an "overhead" expense by your management? Do internal customers get a say in whether they pay your team? Maybe they pay using a consumption-based model — the number of users, applications, devices, or assessments. Maybe your income is based on donations, endowments, or other "goodwill" sources. Maybe your income is a combination of all these. Regardless, your income is part of some pie of money, and you need to know the recipe for the pie.

Once you know where the income originates, consider how you spend it. How much goes to head count and related costs?

How much goes to software, licensing, hardware, training, and other stuff? Which parts of these costs are largely fixed, such as salaries, and which parts are variable, such as training, travel, and so on? Make friends with your finance/accounting partners; they will know how the company categorizes and tracks expenses and will help you to evaluate spending at the right level. Will Larsen's book *An Elegant Puzzle: Systems of Engineering Management* is a great resource to help you think about this.

Lastly, consider your team, function, and service. Are you working efficiently and at a high maturity level? Are you just starting to build the function and need financial support for growth? Are you appropriately resourced to meet the customer demands for your service now and three years from now?

If you have enough income to support your existing team and your future plans, then you're sitting pretty. Now your job is to continue to show the organization the value they are receiving for their investment. However, if you have a gap, you'll need to find ways to fill it. For junior leaders, this usually means talking with your immediate manager/team leader, whose job is to find these funds for you. Find out what they need from you to make a case for getting more funds.

Funding a Program

If you're running a security team with multiple security services and needs, you have the job of getting funding for everything in your security organization. This is no easy task, and it will take a lot of your time, all the time. I recommend having a yearly or quarterly personal goal related to financial management. Depending on the year, it might be simply creating a budget from scratch. It might be identifying top vendor partners and optimizing vendor spend. It might be an organizational realignment to find savings or to get ready for the next growth period. There is always something worth doing that will be a multiplier for your entire team.

Just as your junior leaders need to understand their value and gaps in their resource needs, you will need to know all of this for the entire security organization. You will need to include this in your strategic plan. Use your junior leaders to do the basic data gathering for you. Know what your funding priorities are to advance your strategy in support of the business mission. Be able to articulate which items are mission-critical for managing the organization's security risk and which items are experimental growth opportunities.

Unless you are sitting on a pile of money, you will have to go to different groups and places to ask for funds. Consider the information in the following sections.

Self-Funding

You should always be looking for ways to self-fund security spending. Typically, this comes from automating processes to free up resources to do other work. You could renegotiate vendor contracts to release funds for other purposes. You could redirect the backfilling of head count from sunsetting services to emerging services. You should take care of this first before going to other places for income. Even if you look for self-funding opportunities and can't find any, the act of looking will show your management chain that you are a good steward of company resources.

Usage-Based Income

Some security leaders structure their products so that they charge "by the drink." This is a direct, obvious fee-for-use structure. Be careful with this approach because it encourages people to opt out of using security services, which they tend to do when budgets are tight. From a philosophical perspective, consider whether you think people should be able to "choose" your services. If so, then maybe a usage-based fee structure is worth considering.

Continuous/Permanent Funding

Sometimes, you need to ask for support to create, maintain, or grow an existing operational function. This can't be done with a one-time dump of cash. It needs to be committed to as an ongoing organizational cost. Ongoing operational costs don't remain constant year over year, even if the head count and tools do. The cost of security employees rises every year. If you have to do a replacement hire, it will cost you more than your existing head count. Licensing costs can grow with the number of widgets (head count or devices). So, as you think about your operational costs, plan at least three years into the future, taking into account growth, employee turnover, and other business inputs.

Project Funding

Sometimes you are still in an experimental phase, trying on a new technology or process. Here, you can ask for a one-time fund injection to do a proof of concept, try something new, or get your existing team trained to take on a new challenge. This ask might go to your primary financing group (especially if the project will ultimately increase operational costs), or perhaps you can ask another part of the business that would be a key stakeholder in the project to cost-share a smaller launch.

Shared Costs

Often, some costs can be shared between the security team and other groups. For example, if you're rolling out new application security tools, working with the application development team to divide costs is a perfectly legitimate funding strategy. Let's face it: most security tools and services don't exist in a vacuum. They're driven by the general business and technology strategy of the organization. So, make sure you're at the table (or as close to it as you can get) for any strategy planning meetings, and make sure the cost of security services is included in that planning.

Vendor Investments

Often, a vendor will be willing to invest services or licenses to help move the needle along for you. Don't overlook these strategic partnerships as a source of funds. If you're willing to lock yourself into a multiyear purchasing contract, you might get a cheaper product over the life of the agreement, either through a reduction in license cost or through a "free" bank of licenses to use. However, be careful with vendors who are offering something for free. Nothing is free. Often, these kinds of offers come with higher back-end or renewal costs, or they create integration costs that you bear. Consider these options, but make sure you manage for those hidden expenses.

Grants

Depending on your industry, you might be able to apply for grants to provide seed funding for a project or initiative. Some larger companies offer innovation grants for their internal staff. Perhaps there are state or federal funding grants to hire people in cybersecurity jobs. Consider these kinds of income to be one-time use only, but don't overlook them!

Major Company Initiatives

Your technology and business partners will have their own major projects and initiatives, and it is likely that your team will be asked to support their initiative somehow. Take the opportunity to ask that project team for funding to support your team's costs. This could be funding for additional head count, licenses, or services.

The Big Ask

Once you've identified potential funding sources, then you need to go ask for the money. The typical format for asking for money, regardless of the source, is as follows:

- **Define the problem:** Here is your opportunity to tell a story. What is the business problem you're trying to address? Is it an old risk, a new threat, a compliance problem, or a competitive advantage issue? If you can, tie it to the mission of the people you're presenting to.
- **Remind them of the good work you've done in the past:** You don't have to spend a lot of time here, but a subtle reminder of how well you've managed things in the past will help establish credibility and settle any nerves about spending more money.
- **Describe the potential solution:** There might be more than one solution, but make sure that any option you give them is one you can live with. A low-balled solution is often worse than no solution at all, so don't make the lowest-cost option a bad option. Describe the solution in functional terms (how it would work and who would run it), and consider the impact to stakeholders (customers, IT staff, or others).
- **Outline the risks of not getting the resources:** This is where knowing your audience is so important. The risks need to be meaningful to the decision-makers. If possible, you need to make the risks appear urgent without using fear,

uncertainty, and doubt (FUD). People are motivated to act based on how imminent they think a bad thing is, so help them understand how this solution will help you *today*, even if the solution is intended to address a future threat.

- **Detail the costs of the solution(s) and how your team has worked to self-generate these funds elsewhere:** Leadership wants to know you're committed to this, and they want to know what this will cost them to join in.
- **Describe the outcome in business terms, not just security terms, and describe why it will be great:** End on a positive note. Yes, there is a threat, and yes, it will take resources to address it. But if you do things right, it will help in lots of areas, not just security.
- **Finish with the ask:** Leave them with the question you need answered. Be explicit and clear on what you need and when.

Know the data behind the numbers, and be prepared to use that data to support your request. Also, know that you can't walk into a room cold and expect to get a warm reception. Your job as a leader is to build partnerships and credibility with leadership continuously. If you do that, the entity from whom you are requesting the funds will already know your strategies and needs. Often, funds can come from unlikely quarters, so be prepared to be engaged in funding conversations with many stakeholders throughout the year.

What's Next?

- Gather your numbers. Know the sources of income and how you spend it.
- Gather your options. Talk to other leaders and finance people at your company about how they get funding and what the options are for you.

- Know your stakeholders. Who authorizes you to spend money, and who makes it happen? Often, they are not the same people. You will need relationships with all of them. What are their risk and spending constraints?
- Review your strategy. What do you want to do in the short, medium, and long term, and how much will that cost?
- Draft up your financial plan. To the extent that you can, share it with mentors, networks, or other helpers. Sense-check with your manager.

CHAPTER

22

How Do I Talk About My Security Program?

Summary

- **Start with a story:** Use data and benchmarks to support your story, but don't lead with them.
- **Focus on the future:** The past is history. Focus on what you need today and tomorrow. Build on the past only if it helps your future story.
- **Communicate well and often:** Control the narrative; otherwise, people will create their own.

When we become leaders of a security program, we usually come to the role with no training on presenting a business case or sharing the work of the security program with the organization. It doesn't occur to most of us how much we would need to have this skill. Wouldn't the program just speak for itself? Short answer: no.

For some of us, our first instinct is to use metrics to talk about our programs. We search for "security metrics" or go to security analyst websites or conference talks about metrics. Board members, chief financial officers (CFOs), and other metrics-driven people need metrics. There is a completely valid school of thought that says, "You cannot manage what you cannot measure." A great book on this topic is *How to Measure Anything in Cybersecurity Risk* by Douglas Hubbard and Richard Seiersen.

Over time, I found the metrics approach to be insufficient. It certainly worked in some places, like when asking for more money from the CFO, but often it was too weedy for everyone else. No one cared, really, about how old our vulnerabilities were, how many vendor products we had reviewed, or how many policies we'd cross-walked our framework to. As the CISO, these were all operationally important to me, but talking about this put everyone else to sleep.

Your role as a security leader is to get the organization to invest in the security program and culture. To do this, you need to generate the interest of the community in security things. You need to get them to care about security as much as you do. You do this by telling stories.

What Story Should I Tell?

These days, most security leaders must spend some of their time representing their program to organizational leadership — the

C-suite, the risk committee, or the board. In all cases, there is a need to explain: What are you doing? Is it working? Is it good enough compared to peer organizations? Is it efficient? For many CISOs, this is *really hard*.

There is no cookie-cutter way to talk about security with leadership. There are plenty of resources available to give you PowerPoint templates about how to do a security presentation, but the way to present to leadership will be as varied as the organization itself. If a company cares most about efficiency, then the security program *must* cover how security is efficient. If the company cares about being on the bleeding edge of technology, then the security team must also be there, and the presentation must highlight this. If you need to ask for a ton of money, then the presentation must actively make a case for requesting money.

Each presentation will take time to craft and will be unique. Some things will be common across all of them, all the time, as you will learn in the coming sections.

Build Credibility

Every time a security leader makes a presentation, the credibility of the presenter is one of the things being evaluated. For the security leader, this means that the audience needs to walk away trusting that the program is in good hands, that the security leader knows their stuff, and that even when times are tough, the organization will be well-placed to deal with it because of the security leader.

How do you build credibility?

- **Indicate that you understand the business you're in.** Don't just dive into vulnerability metrics or incident reports. Recognize the current business challenges organizational leadership cares about. Is it a public company that cares about share price? Find a way to link the introduction of the security program to market performance. Does the company produce security products? Highlight the use of security products with the success (or failures) of the security program.

- **Know how you compare to peers and competitors.** Benchmarking is your (temperamental) friend. Conversations with the board always include comparisons with how other similar organizations are doing in terms of spending, incidents, tool usage, and so on. Are you spending more or less than your peers? How's the industry looking compared to your own company? What do external auditors say about your program?
- **Demonstrate knowledge of security trends.** This takes two forms: threats to your organization and adoption of new tools/techniques to address issues. Find ways to link the programs and services you have to the current issues of the day. For example, are you dealing with ransomware? Discuss current ransomware events in your industry, how your program addresses those issues, and where you need to take your program to get and stay ahead of the problem.
- **Know your audience.** This is critical, particularly when you're dealing with a board. If you are presenting to a CFO who cares about spending, be prepared to address spending in your presentation. Minimally, be prepared to answer any questions. If your board members come from other industries, know what is happening in their world, too, and make sure that you relate it back to your own program. Got someone who cares about how the customer will respond? Talk about how your program supports the customer. Whether you are presenting to an internal group, a board, or external

stakeholders, take the time to do your homework and know where they will have interests and concerns. Be prepared to address those interests and concerns.

Know Your Money

There is always (always!) a consideration of resources in all of these presentations. For an internal group, the question might be, "How much will this cost?" For a board, the question might be, "Are we devoting enough resources to security?" (Typically, the answer is "no.") Rarely, internal security is seen as a strategic differentiator. (If you work for a security product company, this might be different.) That means even if you have a fabulous program, there will always be two underlying questions: "Is it worth it?" and "Can we afford this?" If you work for an organization that devotes money to security and has an established program, the question is often, "Are we spending our money effectively?" There is no escaping this question.

To answer the money question, you need to have a macro and micro view.

The macro view is these overarching questions: How much do you spend on security? And is it enough? Again, go back to benchmarking. There are usually two metrics thrown at this question. Many security leaders hate these metrics, so feel free to take or leave them, but you should at least know them:

- Security spend as a percentage of information technology (IT) spend
- Security spend as a percentage of revenue

A quick internet search will usually give you benchmarks within the last couple of years. You will also find metrics on whether peers plan to increase, decrease, or keep flat their security spending. Do your best to make this apply in your context. I recognize that often these metrics are "apples to marsupials," but you can make some generalizations about your industry ("Highly regulated industries spend more on security as a percentage of spend") and across your peers ("In our sector, we are in the top X-percentile of spending as a percentage of revenue").

The micro view is used when you're asking for money for a security product or service. Traditional measures of return on investment (ROI) don't work in security because it's hard to make a direct correlation between a security service and an increase in sales/revenue. The best case is that you deal in cost avoidance, but even that is tricky if you make a large investment in a defensive security tool that results in nothing happening!

So, when making a presentation about a current or future product/service, be clear on how you, the security leader, measure value. Feel free to take the time to train the listeners on how security people measure value. (Doing so will build your credibility.) Does it make your security more proactive (which is seen as a good thing by most leaders)? Does it reduce the need to work with lots of vendors, or does it simplify the incident response process? Will it be the first step in enabling the organization to move to a zero-trust model? You still might have to discuss the hard dollars involved in the investment, but the benefits can be about "softer" things, such as improving the risk profile of the organization, reducing the attack surface, and so on.

If you've never studied finance or accounting, now is the time to learn. I'm not suggesting you invest in a Master of Business Administration degree, but find some training that will help you understand company finances and how security fits in.

Be Future-Focused

Whatever happened in your security program or the security industry is in the past. If your company has survived the past, talking about the past in your presentation is useful only if it informs the future. There's no need to dwell on the past. What do you need now, and what will you need tomorrow? What is happening in the industry today, and what is likely to be coming?

A security leader is most often valued for their ability to bring the organization safely forward, not for fixing the gate after the horse has bolted. So, when talking about your security program, it's okay to brag about the great work your team has done only if you translate that into how they'll be great when future things happen. It's okay to discuss security incidents that have happened (and if they've happened directly to your organization, you'll be talking about them a lot!), but the focus should be on the steps you are taking now to make sure the future doesn't repeat the past.

Be Transparent

This is likely the most difficult part of talking about security in your organization.

On the one hand, you must be positive, upbeat, confident, and enabling. Why? Because if you're continually bringing people down, scaring them with reality, or focusing on the negative, they will lose confidence in you and will tune you out. You will lose your ability to lead effectively.

On the other hand, you cannot sugarcoat issues. Your job is to make sure leaders in the organization know the security risks they face and to allow them to address those risks (or accept them and do nothing). This is not your call to make; it is theirs.

Further, it is your job to make sure they know those risks. Hiding them will not serve you or the company well, ever.

So, how can you be positive, upbeat, and confident when you are aware of scary things happening in your organization that need to be addressed?

- If your organization has a risk or compliance committee, these are the places to bring your concerns first. Give those committees the opportunity to understand, evaluate, and respond to the problem. If there isn't a risk or compliance committee, create an "advisory board" (or something like it) for security, and ask committee members to provide "guidance," not "decisions." These "guidance recommendations" can then be used when bringing the issue to leadership groups or the board.
- Always come with a solution or a way of arriving at a solution (even if a request for more funding accompanies that solution). Don't just show up with a problem and dump-and-run. Be the person who can solve the problem, too.
- Don't ask people to fix issues if their role doesn't give them the authority to act. It's okay to allude to issues with these people, but make sure you're not asking someone for support or decisions if they can't fix the problem. In other words, know who has authority in your organization and be strategic about raising issues to them.
- If you must discuss the negative, do so with facts, not emotion. For example, if patching rates are not what you think they should be and are increasing your organizational risk, discuss the data with the operations staff, and then provide options for the decision-makers. Don't throw other parts of the organization under the bus.

- Be pragmatic. Don't ask for perfection when you know full well that perfection isn't impossible. You should expect decisions that are good enough but not perfect, and you will need to champion the team's efforts that, through no fault of their own, cannot comply with your requirements. When presenting to leadership, be pragmatic about the organization's capabilities while you are being optimistic about its ability to rise to the challenges of the security environment.

Be Visible

Regardless of your presentation schedule, you must be prepared to talk about your program — all the time. To be credible with your team and your community, you must constantly share what you know, how you're handling issues, and where you're headed. Find ways to work with communications teams to generate newsletters, team emails/chat notices, and other ways of putting security work front and center of everyone's mind. This is doubly true with senior leadership and the board. If there are industry events happening, use them as a reason to reach out and explain how your security program is dealing with similar issues. If the Federal Bureau of Investigation/ Information Sharing and Analysis Center sends out a warning bulletin, share with senior leaders about how you're addressing the issue.

Telling Stories

Now you have all these pieces, but how do you put them together?

A security leader must create an overarching narrative for the security program and make sure any presentation aligns to that narrative — overtly referencing it where possible. Perhaps you are starting a new program from scratch. If so, then there are lots of ways to tell stories about being on a journey — why the program is needed, why the focus is on certain security tools, and how everyone can be on the journey together. Perhaps you've had a security program for a while, and now you're starting a new phase or focus. Talk about what has changed that is making this new phase necessary. Celebrate where you've come from and leverage those strengths for the next phase. Perhaps you're maintaining an existing top-notch program. Talk about what makes it great, why it remains necessary, and how the community can continue to support that work.

In all cases and in all presentations, start with the story first, not the data or metrics. Ground your program in the values you want the organization to demonstrate. Give examples of work being done well. Talk about peers or competitors who have not done what you are doing and their impact on their organizations. Paint the picture you want them to see. Reuse those images. A story told repeatedly becomes part of the organization's DNA in a way that transitory metrics and data never will.

Remind people of their accomplishments and yours. Emphasize the teamwork between the security team and other parts of the organization. Put the accomplishments in terms of company values, such as partnership, efficiency, innovation, and so on. Don't just talk in terms of security controls.

> People will create a story about your program, regardless of whether you do, so you want to control the narrative.

You can learn what people think by asking them. Do they think security is an administrative hurdle? Do they think breaches are inevitable and there is nothing they can do to stop them? Do they think that the organization is managing security risk well? Are people asking to learn more about security things, or are you forcing security training upon them? If you ask them to use adjectives to describe security in your organization, what adjectives do they choose?

Using stories about the behaviors and programs you want to emulate will make it easier for the people in your organization to see and act upon your vision. Once you've aligned them to your way of thinking, only then can you throw metrics, data, and tactical stuff at them.

What's Next?

- Think about the story you want people to know about your program. Is it a story of growth? Renewal? Sustained professionalism? What is their role in the program? What is your role? What outcomes do you want? Write down your story.
- Talk to your organization about their impressions of the security program. What adjectives do they use? Which ones align with your story, and which ones need to change?
- What images and anecdotes can you use to support your story? Make a list and refer to it often in your presentations. Repetition is your friend.
- Your security program is a brand. Create it, nurture it, and sell it. If you have marketing or communications people to help you, great! If not, find a mentor with marketing skills who can help you think through how to do this.

CHAPTER

23

What Is My Legacy?

Summary

- **Know yourself:** Think about what kind of impact you want to make.
- **Network:** Use your network to learn how others have made their marks on their companies or industries.
- **Communicate well and often:** Have a succession plan, and make sure leadership knows it.

At some point in your career, you will start to think about the long-term impact of your work. You won't just think, "Did I do a good job today?" Instead, you think, "When I leave this job, what will remain? What will people remember me for?" It's never too late to start thinking about this, regardless of your age or experience. Thinking about the legacy of your work will force you to make decisions and strategies that are more impactful to your team, your organization, and you.

In the security profession, leadership doesn't seem to last very long. Conventional wisdom suggests that the average tenure of a chief information security officer (CISO) is about two years, although this is growing. One of the impacts of a short tenure is that a CISO has little time to establish a strong team or create a program that has a long-lasting impact on the organization. A leader who bounces from role to role or from company to company eventually gets to a place where they question the value of the work they are doing, and they ask, "What is my legacy?"

It helps to think about your purpose for leadership. I recommend *One Piece of Paper: The Simple Approach to Powerful, Personal Leadership* by Mike Figliuolo to help you think this through. It will help you think about why you want to lead a program, how you lead a team, and how you share your vision with the broader community. Spend time thinking and learning about yourself this way because it will help you clarify your purpose — both short-term and long-term — and help you focus on the most important things to you.

When you read organizational management books, creating a team is often presented as a carefully planned and methodical endeavor. In this perfect world, a team grows in response to demand from customers and stakeholders, and the leader is ever so intentional about who is in it and how it operates. An organization is most often created and maintained in the real world based on the leader's personality. Sometimes teams and functions are intentionally created, and sometimes a reorganization results in new team members and new functions being added to a portfolio. A strong leader attracts more responsibility, resulting in new and different functions being added to an already growing work stable. Personality-driven organizational design is much more the rule than the exception.

You can see this happen in the real world. A leader will join or start a team, and it will grow. The team is highly engaged and high functioning, and it delivers a lot of valuable solutions and does some fun work. The leader invests time and emotion into the team and is proud of the work they do. Then the leader leaves, and it takes about a year for the team to be split up and shared among other leaders. It isn't the fault of the new team leader that this occurred. Instead, it is the old leader's lack of understanding on how to lead the team (and stakeholders) so that the remaining team members continue the work after the leader leaves. Their lack of preparation leaves the team exposed to organizational pressures. Few people understand what potential remains if the team was kept together, so leadership decides not to keep the team together.

As you move into a leadership role, you will see that you have two kinds of lasting effects: your personal image and reputation within the broader security industry and the impact of your team on your immediate company. Some leaders spend time on only one of those areas. They invest a lot of time in industry events, mentoring, and so on, or they spend time only on their own companies and never attend industry events. The best leaders spend time in both areas. As you think about your role — your work, your team, and your impact on your organization — can you say that it is "sticky"? Do you think people will remember the value you've brought to the team, organization, and industry? Will they build on that value?

Making an Impact on the Industry

There are luminaries in the security world — people who are thought leaders, inventors, and mentors who show the way to the rest of us. Most of us won't be those people. However, most of us can carve out a niche where we are and have a lasting impact, regardless of the individual jobs we hold throughout our careers. Being a leader at an organization often gives us the time and platform to show leadership outside the organization. Being a leader in the industry allows you to have a continuous positive effect despite the ups and downs of our day jobs. If you want to leave a legacy, consider the following:

- **Develop security talent in your local region:** This can be done through local professional chapters, one-on-one mentoring, or the creation of an internship program. This can help you in a variety of ways. The people you assist spread out like ripples in a pond, and they go on to other security companies and organizations. Assisting these folks not only helps them, but gives you some personal insight into the things they are learning. These folks become part of your own hiring pipeline, improving the talent in your immediate team and improving the general talent in the industry, which helps us all. Conversations with a circle of up-and-coming talent keeps you in touch with their thinking, experiences, and needs, which will help you with managing your own team. Your definition of "local region" can be as small or large as you want. There are plenty of opportunities to help with capture the flag and other state, regional, or training events. You can just as easily mentor someone from your hometown as you can mentor someone in another state. Think about helping people who are trying to get into security, as well as those who are already in the profession. The goal here is to help them gain the confidence and skills to take charge of their careers, so think of this as a service opportunity.
- **Teach security/risk at a local school such as a high school, community college, or university:** Schools are

always looking for experienced practitioners to share their knowledge. While teaching can be a time-consuming new skill to learn, it is so rewarding. These students know little about the security profession or how it works, and there are plenty of opportunities to give them new skills and present them with new opportunities that they would not otherwise have learned or had. Their enthusiasm is contagious, and the simple act of teaching will help you hone your own skills. You can get started by talking to other security people who do this already or by reaching out directly to schools to see what opportunities exist. Many security networking organizations already send security people in to schools, so check those programs out as a starting point.

- **Serve on nonprofit boards:** Typically, nonprofit board representation is an unpaid, volunteer position. Service on these boards is a great way to learn about board leadership and function. Our nonprofit partners really need security help, so taking time to serve on a board is a great way to give back to the community. Your presence can help grow general community understanding about security issues. Board leadership positions are sometimes gained by word of mouth and sometimes are posted publicly. Again, talk to your security network to find people who serve on boards to find out how they took on a position. Even your security networking organization has a board, so perhaps you can volunteer there.
- **Serve on for-profit boards:** These positions are more difficult to attain and are often available based on reputation and word of mouth. Often, they are paid positions. Spend some time researching for-profit boards in your location. Many for-profit companies (and regulators) recognize the need to have a security professional on the board, so you

might see opportunities open for these roles. Consider that many who serve on for-profit boards also serve on multiple boards. If you can help them better understand security on one board, this understanding will transfer to their leadership of other companies — even if those boards don't have a security subject-matter expert (SME).

- **Invest deeply in one security area:** Becoming an SME in one area of security can be a meaningful way to give back to the industry. Let's face it, the security profession is getting bigger and bigger every day, and there is an increasing number of functional areas of expertise. If you're into analysis and knowledge creation, pick your topic of choice, and go deep. Tell people about what you've learned, create user groups focused on that one topic, and spread the word.
- **Engage with national groups to improve the industry:** You can do this by engaging through threat intelligence sharing or by working with Information Sharing and Analysis Centers (ISACs) and Information Sharing and Analysis Organizations (ISAOs) or policy think tanks. These groups are looking for experienced security practitioners to help grow their influence and improve their impact. Being a voice for the industry can be a great way to leave a legacy and open partnership doors. The things you learn in these partnerships are immediately applicable to your day job, so while it's an investment of time, it also has an immediate and long-term impact.
- **Consider focusing on a subgroup who needs additional support:** This includes minorities, women, veterans, foster kids, low-income students, and so on. These groups need support with everything from skills development to interview practice. Conversely, hiring managers need help understanding how to engage these groups inclusively

and equitably. Your work with these groups will help you be a better leader and will expand your hiring pipeline, so yet again, there is an immediate and long-term benefit to this work. There are plenty of places to engage to help these groups arrive and thrive in security, and the industry could use all the help it can get!

Making an Impact on Your Company

If your work is going to continue even after you've left the company, there are things you need to be doing now to pave the way for that work to continue. First, impacting the company means that the core team is identified as a value-adding unit. People should be able to say, "Because of the security team, we were able to do X," and "We need the security team to do Y." The security team should be able to look backward and say, "We did that," and look forward to say, "We can do the next thing, too." Collectively, the organization and the security team should be able to see that things are better because of security, not despite it. So how do you get there?

- **Succession planning:** Make sure every role you and your team play has someone trained to step in after you leave. As a team leader, it is particularly important to have a personal successor. Identify someone who has the talent to step into your role. Make sure your management chain knows how much confidence you have in that individual (or individuals). If you have a large team, you might have more than one person in mind. Give your successor assignments that highlight their readiness. The point is to make sure your stakeholders know that just because you're leaving doesn't mean the structure of the team needs to change dramatically. This also means ensuring that your individual functions and services are strong and work well as a collective unit. If they are perceived as unsupported, siloed, weak, or ineffective, they will likely be removed, changed, or absorbed by other groups.

- **Promote team successes:** Whenever your team has a "win," make sure you're talking about it in terms of the success of the team, not in terms of your personal success. "Look what the team did!" is much better. At every opportunity, make sure you're promoting the value of the team, not the individuals and not you. Link the team successes to the values and objectives of your company. Make sure people other than you are also promoting the security team. Make it clear that the team is stronger together and weaker apart.
- **Promote the team journey:** You are *never* done with security; there will always be more to do. Make sure you have a team strategy, a team roadmap, and a team plan to get there. Make sure your superiors and stakeholders understand that the team is necessary to complete the roadmap and that the roadmap is necessary to make the organization successful. This will support the continued work of the team. Even if the team gets aligned to another group or leader, the goal is to keep the team generally functioning together.
- **Promote the team history:** While you must always be future and opportunity-oriented, you also must not forget the value the team has added previously. Continue to celebrate wins. Remind people that wins are built on top of other achievements — they don't happen in isolation. Remind stakeholders that they need to keep building on top of the existing team and not instead of starting from scratch elsewhere.

For some of us, showing up each day, working hard, and not worrying about a legacy is completely normal and appropriate. If this is you, great! Finding long-term meaning in our efforts is an important part of our professional growth for the rest of us. If we're going to spend all this time at work, it should count for something bigger than ourselves.

What's Next?

How do you impact your industry? First, decide where you want to spend your time in teaching, board service, or thought leadership, and then do the following:

- Find people who are doing what you want to do and ask them how they got to where they are.
- Reach out to networking groups that can help you on this journey.
- Be prepared to invest time in this outside your day job — this will be in addition to your normal role.
- Give yourself a target — things to do/achieve in the next six months. Work that plan.

How do you do impact your company?

- Continue to be a partner for company leadership and your strategic partners.
- Create a succession plan for your role, and make sure your team and management chain understand it.
- Give your successor a chance to get in front of leadership wherever possible. Be intentional about the projects and

initiatives you give to your successor. Let them demonstrate their capabilities.

- Keep your strategic roadmap front and center for conversations with leadership. Remind them often of where you're headed, where you are on the journey, and what's coming next. Emphasize the role of the team when you talk about your strategy.

Epilogue

Often, I walk away from mentoring meetings having learned something new or having been reminded of something I've long forgotten. It's always a joy and always useful for me. Ideally, it's useful for those I mentor.

Covering the questions that span a whole security career is impossible. In this book, I've tried to address the common ones — the ones that people most often ask and most often seem to struggle with. Each question area raises several follow up questions, so I hope I've addressed some of those, too.

The role of a mentor is never to give the answers; instead, it's to help the mentee to learn how to find the answers on their own. It's about helping them know how to frame the questions and how to think about the problems. It's about giving them context — why the issue exists and what factors contribute to the problem. In this book, I've attempted to do this for you, too; I've tried to give you the "why" in a general way, so you can find your own why and answer these questions for yourself.

A mentor helps others find their own answers because what worked for the mentor won't always work again. Being successful in any profession, particularly security, requires self-awareness. You need to know what motivates you to do this work and how your work environment fosters your spirit. Throughout this book, I have provided many resources to help you find the answers as you dig deeper into your particular problem. Many people in the security industry stand ready to help you. I hope I have helped you find them.

I reached out to my network to get their opinions and experiences and incorporated them into this book. The support and input from my security community reminded me how much I love the people I work with and how much I admire all they do, all the time. So many people made invaluable recommendations. So many of them just said, "Let me know how I can help."

I hope that wherever you are on your security path, you find the security guides to walk with you for a while. I hope that you learn from them and share what you learned with others.

Happy travels.

Appendix: Resources

The books and resources I have listed next are ones that have helped me think about some of the topics I've discussed. Some of them were page-turners, some of them were as dry as toast, but all of them had some nugget that helped the people I mentor (or me) progress on their security paths.

Books

- *One Piece of Paper: The Simple Approach to Powerful, Personal Leadership* by Mike Figliuolo
- *Start with Why* by Simon Sinek
- *Confident Cyber Security: How to Get Started in Cyber Security and Future Proof Your Career* by Dr. Jessica Barker
- *The Pentester Blueprint: Starting a Career as an Ethical Hacker* by Philiip L. Whylie and Kim Crawley
- *Emotional Intelligence* by Daniel Goleman
- *Crucial Conversations: Tools for Talking When the Stakes Are High* by Kerry Patterson, Joseph Grenny, Ron McMillan, and Al Switzler
- *What Got You Here Won't Get You There: How Successful People Become Even More Successful* by Marshall Goldsmith

- *On Writing Well* by William Zinsser
- *Good Is Not Enough: And Other Unwritten Rules for Minority Professionals* by Keith Wyche
- *What Works: Gender Equality by Design* by Iris Bohnet
- *Now, Discover Your Strengths* by Marcus Buckingham and Donald O. Clifton
- *The Manager's Path: A Guide for Tech Leaders Navigating Growth and Change* by Camille Fournier
- *An Elegant Puzzle: Systems of Engineering Management* by Will Larsen
- *The Secret Thoughts of Successful Women: Why Capable People Suffer from Imposter Syndrome and How to Thrive In Spite of It* by Valerie Young
- *CISO Compass* by Todd Fitzgerald
- *Strategy Maps* by Robert S. Kaplan and David P. Norton
- *The First 90 Days: Proven Strategies for Getting Up to Speed Faster and Smarter* by Michael D. Watkins
- *How to Measure Anything in Cybersecurity Risk* by Douglas Hubbard and Richard Seiersen

Networking Organizations and Conferences

- BSides Conferences: www.securitybsides.com
- International Systems Security Association (ISSA): www.issa.org
- Women in Cybersecurity (WiCys): www.WiCys.org
- International Consortium of Minority Cybersecurity Professionals (ICMCP): www.icmcp.org

Certification Organizations

- (ISC)2: www.ISC2.org
- SANS Institute: www.SANS.org
- ISACA: www.ISACA.org
- Cloud Security Alliance: www.cloudsecurityalliance.org

Podcasts

- Risky Business: https://Risky.biz
- CISO Series: https://cisoseries.com
- Hacker Valley Studio Podcast: https://hackervalley.com
- The Cyber Ranch: https://Hackervalley.com/cyberranch/
- The CyberWire: https://thecyberwire.com/podcasts
- Smashing Security: https://smashingsecurity.com

Other Resources

- The Cyber Canon: For peer-reviewed security books (https://icdt.osu.edu/cybercanon)
- Cyberseek.org: For U.S.-based information about security job roles and statistics
- NIST NICE Career Framework: https://niccs.us-cert.gov/nice-cybersecurity-workforce-framework-work-roles
- Cybersecurity Mindmaps: http://rafeeqrehman.com/
- Leslie Carhart: Starting an Infosec Career https://tisiphone.net/2015/10/12/starting-an-infosec-career-the-megamix-chapters-1-3/

- Danier Meissler: How to Start an Infosec Career https://danielmiessler.com/blog/build-successful-infosec-career/
- Hacking Training: https://TheCyberMentor.com
- Pluralsight Training: https://pluralsight.com
- LinkedIn Learning: https://LinkedIn.com/learning
- HackTheBox: https://hackthebox.eu
- Verizon Data Breach Investigations Report: https://enterprise.verizon.com/resources/reports/dbir

About the Author

Helen E. Patton is an advisory CISO at Cisco, where she shares security strategies with the security community. Previously she spent eight years as the CISO at The Ohio State University, where she was awarded the 2018 ISE North American Academic/ Public Sector Executive of the Year. Before joining Ohio State, she spent 10 years in risk and resiliency at JPMorgan Chase.

Helen actively encourages collaboration across and within industries to enable better information security and privacy practices. She believes in improving diversity and inclusion in the workforce and mentors people interested in pursuing careers in security, privacy, and risk management. She advocates for more naps and is anti-bagpipes.

Helen has a master's degree in public policy and has earned various industry certifications. She serves on the State of Ohio CyberOhio Advisory Board, the Manufacturing and Digital USA Cybersecurity Advisory Board, and the Ohio State University College of Electrical and Computer Engineering Industry Advisory Board. She is a faculty member for the Digital Director's Network and for the Educause Leadership Institute.

Acknowledgments

To my amazing colleagues who took the time to pre-read my drafts and help me craft a coherent story: Steve Romig, Dan Walsh, Adrian Sanabria, Joanna Grama, David Seidl, Rob Duhart, and Marissa Ball.

To my Ohio State security colleagues for being my teachers and friends: Gates Garrity-Rokous, Steve Romig, Gary Clark, Rich Nagle, Holly Drake, Amber Buening, and everyone who breathes "Security and Trust" daily. Thank you for keeping me sane.

Gratitude to my Cisco team, Wendy Nather, Dave Lewis, Richard Archdeacon, and Wolf Goerlich, who allow me the space to think out loud, without a filter.

Thanks to the #Tinkertribe, who encourage and connect me to good things when I need them most: Gary Hayslip, Chris Castaldo, Yael Nagler, Allan Alford, Jules Okafar, Will Lin, Brian Markham, Adrian Sanabria, Dan Walsh, Andy Ellis, and a host of others!

For my Columbus, Ohio (and sometimes beyond), security community, who lift me up every single day: Connie Matthews, Don Boian, Marissa Ball, Chris Zell, Samara Williams, Rob Duhart, and Brent Huston.

To my security colleagues on Twitter, Slack, and LinkedIn who keep me informed of the latest in security thinking — for better or worse! There are too many to mention, but they have been so important in my career and personal development.

To anyone who has ever asked to meet me for coffee — virtual or otherwise — to talk about security: I have been amazed at your journey, and you have taught me so much.

Most of all, for my family near and far. Thank you for supporting me as I have worked through my own cybersecurity path and for giving me the space and grace to pursue my personal goals and write this book.

Index

A

Acting quickly, importance of, 153
Active Directory, 57, 207
Active testing, learning about, 100
Ad hoc learning, 102
Allow lists, 231
Analyst resources, as learning option, 104
Appearance, importance of in job searches, 90
Application security, described, 57
Artificial intelligence, 57
Asset management, as example of function, 208

B

Barker, Jessica (author)
- *Confident Cyber Security: How to Get Started in Cyber Security and Future Proof Your Career*, 17, 58, 287

Being intentional, importance of, 119, 129
Benchmarks, use of, 117
Bias
- checking your language for in job postings, 224
- few as being immune to, 121

Block lists, 231
Blogging, value of, 78
Blogs, as learning option, 105
Blue teams, described, 32
Board members, managing yours, 245–246
Bohnet, Iris (author)
- *What Works: Gender Equality by Design*, 288

Books, as resources, 287–288
Boot camps
- as learning option, 104
- as training option, 50

BSides Conferences, 38, 288
Buckingham, Marcus (author)
- *Now, Discover Your Strengths*, 25, 138, 288

Business goals
- aligning reporting to, 200
- being sure functions and structure of team supports your company's, 210

Business priorities, knowing yours, 191–193
Business risk picture, drawing of, 184–185

C

Carey, Marcus J., 5
Carhart, Leslie, 58
Certifications
  consideration of to advance your security career, 135
  list of, 47–48
  organizations for, 289
  truth about security certifications, 46–48
Change agent, as security persona, 23
Chief information security officer (CISO)
  average tenure of, 181, 276
  typical background for, 137
CISA certification, 47, 48
CISM certification, 48, 135
CISO (chief information security officer)
  average tenure of, 181, 276
  typical background for, 137
CISO Compass (Fitzgerald), 288
CISO Series podcast, 289
CISSP certification, 47, 48, 135
Clifton, Donald O. (author)
  Now, Discover Your Strengths, 25, 138, 288
Cloud, moving of technology stack to, 190
Cloud certification, 47
Cloud security, 57
Cloud Security Alliance (website), 289
Cloud security certification, 135
Codes of conduct, lack of commonly understood ones in security, 31
Communication
  importance of communicating well and often, 97, 130, 154, 164, 179, 188, 202, 218, 227, 241, 253, 263, 275
  security people as relying heavily on, 33
Communication skills, 59–62
CompTIA+ certification, 47
Confident Cyber Security: How to Get Started in Cyber Security and Future Proof Your Career (Barker), 17, 58, 287
Core services, as item for strategy, 199
Cover letter, to accompany résumé, 79–80, 87, 90
Crawley, Kim (author)
  The Pentester Blueprint: Starting a Career as an Ethical Hacker, 58, 287
Crucial Conversations: Tools for Talking When the Stakes Are High (Patterson, Grenny, McMillan, and Switzler), 64, 287
Cultural issues, understanding of, 230–231
Culture, do you fit into culture at current job?, 170
Culture change, 122, 192, 199–200
Curiosity, importance of staying curious, 4, 10, 97, 108, 130, 143, 179, 188, 201, 217, 227

Current events
importance in learning about, 101
keeping managers informed of, 249–250
Cyber insurance provider, checking with to identify required functions, 208–209
Cybersecurity mindmaps, 36
Cybersecurity Mindmaps (website), 289
Cyberseek.org, 26, 29, 35, 138, 226, 289
The Cyber Canon (website), 289
The Cyber Ranch podcast, 289
The CyberWire podcast, 289

D
Daniel Meissler: How to Start an Infosec Career (website), 290
Data analytics, 57
Degrees
consideration of to advance your security career, 136
as training option, 50
DEI (diversity, equity, and inclusion) issues, training and awareness materials around, 231
DHCP, 57
Diet, taking care of yourself with, 113
Digital presence, importance of in finding work, 77–78
Diversity
approaches to, 229–230
attracting diverse talent, 232–233
considering "blind" selection processes, 235
defined, 229
encouragement of, 227–239
hashtags to use on social media for, 233
lack of in security workforce, 120
language used in talking about groups of people, 231
leading initiatives for, 125
retaining diverse talent, 236–237
talent pipeline for, 233
and team building, 239
understanding cultural issues regarding, 230–232
writing job description and posting to attract diverse candidate pool, 234–235
Diversity, equity, and inclusion (DEI) issues, training and awareness materials around, 231
DNS, 57

E
Education (including of on résumé), 75
Effective listening, 63–64
EI (emotional intelligence), 62–63
An Elegant Puzzle: Systems of Engineering Management (Larsen), 256, 288
Emotional intelligence (EI), 62–63
Emotional Intelligence (Goleman), 63, 113, 287
Emotional quotient (EQ), 63
Environmental analysis, considering your industry, 190–191
EQ (emotional quotient), 63
Equity issues, paying attention to, 228, 229

Ethical hacking
  learning about, 100
  as red team job, 33
Ethical hacking certification, 47, 48
Exercise, taking care of yourself with, 113
Exit interviews, 239
External analysis, resources for, 196
Extracurricular things (including of on résumé), 75–76

F

Fear, uncertainty, and doubt (FUD), 193, 260–261
Figliuolo, Mike (author)
  One Piece of Paper: The Simple Approach to Powerful, Personal Leadership, 276, 287
Financial support. *See* funding
Firewalls, 57
The First 90 Days (Watkins), 181, 243, 288
Fitzgerald, Todd (author)
  CISO Compass, 288
Flexibility
  importance of, 129
  as key leadership skill, 192
Foundational security, 207–208
Fournier, Camille (author)
  The Manager's Path: A Guide for Tech Leaders Navigating Growth and Change, 151, 288
Four-year degree, as training option, 50
FUD (fear, uncertainty, and doubt), 193, 260–261
Function(s)
  building new ones, 213–214
  discontinuing of, 212–213
  identifying required ones, 208–209
  use of term, 207
Funding
  asking for, 260–261
  continuous/permanent funding, 258
  grants, 259
  having goal related to financial management, 256–257
  importance of in security, 34
  major company initiatives, 259–260
  project funding, 258
  for security program, 254–261
  self-funding, 257
  shared costs, 258–259
  usage-based income, 257–258
  vendor investments, 259
Future, being focused on, 269

G

General business experience, consideration of what you already have, 37–38
GitHub, for demonstrating your coding skills, 78
Goals
  aligning reporting to general business goals, 200
  being sure functions and structure of team supports your company's goals, 210
  changing your personal goal, 139
  determining long-term goals, 168–169

high goals as motivating, 157
related to financial management, 256–257
of team/group, 141, 150, 199
using emotion to achieve, 63
Goldsmith, Marshall (author)
What Got You Here Won't Get You There: How Successful People Become Even More Successful, 151, 287
Goleman, Daniel (author)
Emotional Intelligence, 63, 113, 287
Good Is Not Enough: And Other Unwritten Rules for Minority Professionals (Wyche), 288
Governance, risk, and compliance (GRC)
as nontechnical security term, 33
technical skills taking form of, 57
Governance frameworks, as example of foundational element, 208
GRC (governance, risk, and compliance)
as nontechnical security term, 33
technical skills taking form of, 57
Grenny, Joseph (author)
Crucial Conversations: Tools for Talking When the Stakes Are High, 64, 287

H

Hacker Valley Studio Podcast, 289
Hacking Training (website), 290
HackTheBox (website), 290
Hashtags, diversity hashtags to use on social media, 233
Header and summary (on résumé), 72
Hiring, considering "blind" selection processes in, 235
History, importance of learning about, 101
How to Build a Cybersecurity Career blog (Miessler), 58
How to Measure Anything in Cybersecurity Risk (Hubbard and Seiersen), 264, 288
Hubbard, Douglas (author)
How to Measure Anything in Cybersecurity Risk, 264, 288
Human resource support, importance of in security, 34

I

IAM (Identity and Access Management), adding of to security portfolio, 207
ICMCP (International Consortium of Minority Cyber Professionals), 124, 232, 288
Identity and Access Management (IAM), adding of to security portfolio, 207
Immediate manager, managing yours, 243–244
Imposter syndrome
author's story about, 155–156
dealing with, 153–162
defined, 154
fact-checking your inner monologue, 157–158
keeping track of your successes, 161–162

Imposter syndrome (*Continued*)
knowing competence and incompetence, 158–159
knowing when to ask for help, 159–160
learning and knowing when enough is enough, 160–161
Incident preparation, with leadership team, 247–248
Incident response
as example of foundational element, 208
facilitating user behavior analytics for, 207
learning about issues in, 100, 133
Incident response plan, 248, 250
Inclusivity, fostering of, 229, 232
Information risk, as nontechnical security term, 33
Information Sharing and Analysis Centers (ISACs), 196, 280
Initiative, as professional skill, 65
Intentional career seeker, how to be one, 136–139
Intentionality, importance of, 119, 129
Internal analysis, components of, 196–197
International Consortium of Minority Cyber Professionals (ICMCP), 124, 232, 288
International Systems Security Association (ISSA), 38, 45, 49, 135, 225, 288
Internet of Things (IoT), 56, 57
Internships, as training option, 50
Interviewing
controversy of "testing" candidates' subject-matter knowledge during, 236
exit interviews, 239
recommendations for structure of, 235–236
working on your interviewing skills, 90
IoT (Internet of Things), 56, 57
ISACA, 48, 135, 225, 289
ISACs (Information Sharing and Analysis Centers), 196, 280
(ISC)2, 48, 135, 225, 289
ISSA (International Systems Security Association) (website), 38, 45, 49, 135, 225, 288

J

Jin, Jennifer, 5
Job hopping, 171
Job postings
author's story about, 218–219
on big-name posting boards, 225
challenge of, 220
consideration of where and what you post, 224–225
differentiating between general IT skills and security skills in, 221–222
how to write one, 217–225
including context in, 222–223
language used in, 223–224
skills mismatch as challenge in, 221
Job searches
assessing your efforts so far, 89–92
author's story about, 84
changing roles as a lot of work, 164–165
factors that influence, 83
importance of physical location in, 85

knowing your market, 88–89
looking within your own company for security opportunities, 85–86
as numbers game, 91–92
persistence required for, 82
preparation for, 50
sharpening your skills in, 91
specificity in, 86–87
thinking about your next role, 100–101
Job shadowing, benefits of, 49

K

Kali Linux, 57
Kaplan, Robert S. (author)
Strategy Maps, 288
Kill chains, 243
Knowing your audience, importance of, 81, 266
Knowing yourself, importance of, 9, 19, 30, 41, 53, 81–82, 97, 119, 139, 143, 163, 179, 187, 201, 227, 275

L

Larsen, Will (author)
An Elegant Puzzle: Systems of Engineering Management, 256, 288
Leadership
and management, 145
of security team (*See* security leadership)
working with changes in, 98–99
Learning
ad hoc learning, 102
conferences and professional boot camps, 104
finding best resources for, 99, 103–105
have you learned all you wanted to at current job?, 167–168
importance of, 129
making structured learning plan, 102–103
making time for, 99–101
planned learning, 102
self-study, 104
staying current with security issues and trends, 133
taking a mini-sabbatical for, 103
Legacy, knowing yours, 275–283
Leslie Carhart: Starting an Infosec Career (website), 289
LinkedIn
creating your page in, 77–78, 89
as learning option, 105
making connections via, 135
for placing job postings, 225
use of to find security people to interview, 38
LinkedIn Learning (website), 290
Listening, effectively, 63–64

M

Management
forcing management to understand all that is needed to fund security program, 255
leadership and, 145
middle management as blended role, 149–150
Manager(s)
consideration of being a manager in your security career, 143–151

Manager(s) (*Continued*)
  defined, 147–148
  having regular meetings with, 247
  helping managers understand security, 246–249
  importance of program managers, 34
  importance of project managers, 34
  incident preparation with, 247–248
  keeping them informed of current security events, 249–250
  managing your immediate manager, 243–244
  using security event to get attention of, 250–251
  worst kind of, 148
The Manager's Path: A Guide for Tech Leaders Navigating Growth and Change (Fournier), 151, 288
Marketing groups, security people as relying heavily on, 33
Marketing pitch, practicing of, 90
McMillan, Ron (author)
  Crucial Conversations: Tools for Talking When the Stakes Are High, 64, 287
Mentor
  finding "diamonds in the rough," 228
  role of, 285
Metrics
  author's experience with, 264
  as item for strategy, 199–200
  use of, 117
Middle management, consideration of in your security career, 149–150
Miessler, Daniel, 58
Mindmap(s)
  cybersecurity mindmaps, 36
  defined, 36
  review of, 30, 133
  skills strategy mindmap, 60
Minority. *See also* underrepresented people
  author's story as, 122–123
  being an advocate as, 125–126
  finding workplace allies as, 126–127
  finding your community as, 124–125
  lack of in core technology, security, or risk functions, 229
  leaving particularly stressful roles as, 127–128
  placements of in sales or human resources (HR) or support roles, 229
  reality of minorities working in security, 121
  succeeding as, 119–128
  various statuses as, 120
Miscellaneous resources, 289–290
MITRE ATT&CK Framework, 243
Money
  having macro view of, 267
  having micro view of, 268
Moral crusader, as security persona, 23
"Must do," adding of before "nice to do," 209

N

National Initiative for Cybersecurity Education (NICE) (US), 35, 138, 221, 226
Network zones, 57

Networking
to advance your security career, 134–135
employee groups for, 127
importance of, 48, 91
organizations and conferences for, 288
uses of, 4, 42, 53, 82, 97, 108, 119, 143, 153, 163–164, 179, 187, 201, 217, 227, 253, 275
NICE (National Initiative for Cybersecurity Education) (US), 35, 138, 221, 226
NIST NICE Career Framework (website), 289
Nontechnical security, 33
Norton, David P. (author)
Strategy Maps, 288
Now, Discover Your Strengths (Buckingham and Clifton), 25, 138, 288

O

On Writing Well (Zinsser), 288
One Piece of Paper: The Simple Approach to Powerful, Personal Leadership (Figliuolo), 276, 287
Onion approach, to keeping up with changing security landscape, 99–100
Operational technology (OT) security, as subset of security, 56
Opportunist, being one, 132–136
Organizational change, working with, 99
OSI technology stack, layers of, 56
OT (operational technology) security, as subset of security, 56

P

Partners
benefits of helping ally partners, 126
checking in with trusted partners, 158, 211
creating ones who understand your why as much as you understand theirs as helping with managing your security stress, 118
determining yours as security leader, 182–183
in doing work of security, 33–34
engaging of through creation of incident response plan, 248
existing professionally as being part of larger ecosystem of, 124
fostering security partners, 11
invested in strategy, 189–190
senior-level leaders as best partners when they are bought in, 214
teaching yours why security is important to you, 108
using online or network partners to help you get started, 86
Partnerships
building of as your job as leader, 261

Partnerships (*Continued*)
  building recruiting partnerships, 232
  forming of as professional skill, 64–65
  as requiring skill at listening effectively, 63
Passive testing, learning about, 100
Patterson, Kerry (author)
  Crucial Conversations: Tools for Talking When the Stakes Are High, 64, 287
Penetration tester, as red team job, 32
Penetration testing/pen testing
  learning about, 100
  as red team job, 33
The Pentester Blueprint: Starting a Career as an Ethical Hacker (Wylie and Crawley), 58, 287
People of Color in Technology, 127
Pers Scholars, 233
Phone skills, practicing of, 90
Physical location, importance of in job search, 85
Planned learning, 102
Pluralsight Training (website), 290
Podcasts
  as learning option, 105
  as resources, 289
Presentations
  being focused on future in, 269
  being transparent in, 269–271
  being visible to make them, 271
  building credibility with, 265–267
  including consideration of resources in, 267–268
Principles, leading with, 116–117
Product design, as integral to security ecosystem, 34
Product sales, as integral to security ecosystem, 34
Professional security organizations. *See* (ISC)2; ISACA; ISSA
Professional skills, 59–65
Program managers, importance of in security, 34
Programming language, need for skills in, 57
Project managers, importance of in security, 34
Promotions, in your security career, 139–141
Pronouns, use of, 231
Protector, as security persona, 21, 22
Puzzler, as security persona, 22–23

R

Red teams, described, 32–33
References (including of on résumé), 78–79
Regulations
  having knowledge about, 89, 208–209
  keeping up with changes in, 99
Rehman, Rafeeq, 36
Reporting, as item for strategy, 199–200
Research, opportunities for, 5, 19, 26, 29, 36, 41–42, 71, 129, 232, 234, 235, 279
Resources
  books, 287–288
  certification organizations, 289
  miscellaneous, 289–290

networking organizations and conferences, 288
podcasts, 289
Résumé
bad résumé defined, 69
creation of, 68
elements of, 71–79
good résumé defined, 69
as guide to your future, 68
keywords in, 76–77
linking of to job posting, 70
as not just looking back at your history, 68
purpose of, 69
sharpening of, 87, 89
ways to get yours noticed, 76–77
Reverse engineering, as red team job, 33
Risk
drawing business risk picture, 184–185
information risk as nontechnical security, 33
making sure leaders know security risks they face, 269–270
outlining risks of not getting resources to fund security program, 260–261
security leaders as managing of, 254
Risk assessment
as blue team job, 32
as function, 36
third-party risk assessments, 100
Risk-taking psychology, 111
Risky Business podcast, 289
Roadblocks, in searching for security role, 82
RSS feeds, as learning options, 105

S

SANS Institute (website), 289
SASE (Secure Access Service Edge) architectures, 190
The Secret Thoughts of Successful Women: Why Capable People Suffer from Imposter Syndrome and How Thrive in Spite of It (Young), 161–162, 288
Secure Access Service Edge (SASE) architectures, 190
Security
as always something scary happening in, 117
application security, 57
blessings and challenges in working in, 93
board members as ultimate decision-makers and overseers of, 242
cost of, 110–111
decision-making around, 116
determining your why for wanting career in, 24–28
helping managers understand, 246–249
hiring pipeline for work in, 120
how people are attracted to, 55
as industry not known for diversity, 228
kind of people who do security, 21–24

Security (*Continued*)
knowing why security is valuable, 26–27
lack of commonly understood organizational structure for, 31
no right path to getting into, 42
nonsecurity people as not understanding what it is or what it does, 110
nontechnical security, 33
as not having professional requirement of degrees, skills, or licensing, 31
as often overlooked in name of "customer experience", 115
partners in doing work of, 33–34
as profession that is misunderstood, 20
reasons to pursue career in, 19–27
as relying heavily on communications and marketing groups, 33
technical security, 32–33
as technology function, 55
types of security personas, 21–23
use of term, 13
workforce of as way too homogeneous, 120
Security architecture, as blue team job, 32
Security career
author's story about, 4, 6–13, 84, 122–123, 155–156, 218–219
being an opportunist in, 132–136
being intentional career seeker, 136–139
consideration of managing people in, 143–151
creating progress in, 130–141
deciding if other options are better than your current job, 172–173
deciding if you are being pigeonholed at current job, 169
deciding if you fit into culture at current job, 170
deciding if you have done all you wanted to do at current job, 166–167
deciding if you have learned all you wanted to at current job, 167–168
deciding if you're happy where you are, 165–166
getting promoted, 139–141
job hopping, 171
keeping track of your successes, 161–162
knowing when it's time to move on, 163–173
knowing when to ask for help, 159–160
learning and knowing when enough is enough, 160–161
long-term goals in, 168–169, 182
metaphor of brick wall for, 138
phases of, 131–132
preparing for your next role in, 150–151
staying current with security issues and trends, 133

Security codes of conduct, lack of commonly understood ones, 31
Security controls, as having negative impact on customer experience, 111
Security culture, hierarchy in, 154
Security framework, as item for strategy, 198–199
Security hygiene, 207–208
Security incident response plan, creation of, 248
Security knowledge, pursuit of, 54
Security leadership
  as architect of business's security program, 198
  average tenure of, 181, 276
  building your team, 201–214
  considering focus on subgroup who needs additional support, 280–281
  determining timeline to act, 181
  determining what's on fire, 180
  determining your partners, 182–183
  developing security talent in your local region, 278
  drawing business risk picture, 184–185
  engaging with national groups to improve the industry, 280
  ensuring funding for team, 254–261
  finding strengths and noting weaknesses, 183–184
  having a mandate for, 185–186
  how to manage up, 242–251
  investing deeply in one security area, 280
  knowing how to write job postings, 217–225
  knowing your purpose for, 276
  making impact on your company, 281
  making impact on your industry, 277–278
  managing it strategically, 187–199
  promoting team history, 282
  promoting team journey, 282
  promoting team successes, 282
  providing succession planning, 281–282
  representing your program to organizational leadership, 264–265
  role of, 264
  serving on for-profit boards, 279–280
  serving on nonprofit boards, 279
  starting a new role in, 180
  as storyteller, 271–273
  teaching security/risk at local school, 278–279
Security management, described, 147–148
Security operations, as blue team job, 32
Security organizations. *See* (ISC)2; Information Sharing and Analysis Centers (ISACs); ISACA; ISSA
Security pain points
  addressing of, 194–195
  examples of, 195

Security policy, as nontechnical security term, 33
Security principles, lack of generally accepted ones, 31
Security product companies, 34
Security profession, as young, 31
Security professional
- aligning skills and strengths, 8–9
- challenges in becoming, 14–16
- creating your story as, 8–13
- doing research about, 5, 39
- as evangelist, 109–110
- as having difficulty turning off and getting away from work, 112
- as having to keep things to themselves, 112, 114
- how author became, 4, 6–8
- how to become, 3–17
- interviewing of, 38
- as looking for and finding bad things, 112
- looking for themes of success in, 5
- many as starting in traditional IT fields then moving into security function, 58
- networking, 11–12
- not being perfect, 9–10
- as particularly exposed to being second-guessed, 111
- paying your dues as, 12–13
- shortage of, 14
- staying curious (*See* curiosity)
- staying open to opportunities, 9
- teaching nonsecurity people what they do, 113–114
- what it means to be one, 32–34

Security program
- funding of (*See* funding)
- how to talk about yours, 263–273
- role of security leader as architect of, 198

Security publications, as learning option, 105
Security recruiting firm, consideration of working with, 91
Security strategy
- author's experience with, 192
- creation of, 203
- described, 189
- knowing where roadblocks are likely to be, 193–194

Security stress
- causes of, 113
- management of, 113–118
- as more than usual stress, 112
- as unique, 107, 109–110

Security support functions
- examples of, 210
- importance of, 210–211

Security trends, 190
Seiersen, Richard (author)
- *How to Measure Anything in Cybersecurity Risk*, 264, 288

Self-direction, 146–147
Self-motivation, 146–147
Self-paced training, as training option, 50
Self-promotion, importance of, 91
Self-study, as learning option, 104
Selling yourself, importance of, 67
Senior leaders, managing yours, 244–245
Senior stakeholders, identification of, 242–243

Sinek, Simon (author)
Start with Why, 21, 117, 287
Single contributor, being one, 146–147
Skills
coding skills, 78
communication skills, 59–62
constant honing and learning of, 54
differentiating between general IT skills and security skills in job postings, 221–222
flexibility as key leadership skill, 192
interviewing skills, 90
as listed on résumé, 73–74
phone skills, 90
professional skills, 59–65
in programming languages, 57
soft skills, 74
in technology, 56
Skills strategy mindmap, 60
Slack, as learning option, 105
Sleep, taking care of yourself with, 113, 117–118
Smashing Security podcast, 289
SME (subject-matter expert), 54, 155, 280
Social media
as learning option, 105
use of for job postings, 225, 232
use of to find security people to interview, 38
use of to show active engagement with security community, 90
Soft skills, 74
Start with Why (Sinek), 21, 117, 287
Starting an Infosec Career blog (Carhart), 58
Stories
author's story about security career, 4, 6–13, 84, 122–123, 155–156, 218–219
starting with story when talking about your security program, 263, 264–271
telling of as security leader, 271–273
as unique to individual, 4
writing your own security story, 3, 5–6, 8–13
Strategic planning, as core work of leadership, 188
Strategy
addressing stakeholder pain points, 194–195
attracting supporters to, 194–195
being pragmatic about, 193
consideration of threats and vulnerabilities in, 195–197
as core work of leadership, 188
items to consider when drawing up yours, 198–199
knowing your business priorities, 191–193
partners invested in, 189–190
rinse and repeat cycles of, 197–198
as road map, 188–189
security strategy (*See* security strategy)
Strategy Maps (Kaplan and Norton), 288
Streaming media, as learning option, 105

Stress. *See also* security stress
 causes of, 108
 changes in causes of, 109
 as fixable issue, 108–109
 management of, 113–118
 as not inherently bad, 108
 as positive, 108
Subject-matter expert (SME), 54, 155, 280
Succession planning, 281–282
Support functions
 examples of, 210
 importance of, 210–211
Switzler, Al (author)
 Crucial Conversations: Tools for Talking When the Stakes Are High, 64, 287

T

Tabletop exercises (TTX), creation of to help management chain and leadership understand security, 248–249
Taking care of yourself, importance of, 107
Talent pipeline, 233–234
Team, funding of, 255–256
Team building
 building yours, 201–214
 continuing a great thing, 205–206
 continuing to build a growing thing, 206
 discontinuing a function, 212–213
 fixing a broken thing, 205
 as following creation of strategy, 203
 identifying areas of weakness, 211–212
 identifying important things, 209–211
 as like house building, 214
 from scratch, 204–205
 things to consider in, 207
Team history, promotion of, 282
Team journey, promotion of, 282
Team management, 203
Team successes, promotion of, 282
Technical experience, consideration of what you already have, 36–37
Technical security
 blue teams and red teams, 32–33
 use home security lab to go deep into, 57
Technology
 changes in way people use it, 98
 as entry point to security work, 55–56
 having skills in, 56–58
 keeping up with changes in, 98
Technology stack, moving of to cloud, 190
Thinking, checking yours, 153
Threat hunter, as red team job, 33
Threat intelligence
 as blue team job, 32
 as red team job, 33
Threats
 kinds of, 209–210
 making sure functions help address them, 209
Time management, to make room for learning, 99–101
Training

around diversity, equity, and inclusion (DEI) issues, 231
for full-time nonsecurity worker, 45–46
as growing and changing in security training market, 49
on managing diverse teams, 236
many options for to get in to security, 42
nontraditional student path, 44–45
outside of classrooms, 46–50
of staff as item for strategy, 199
traditional student path, 43–44
types of, 50
Training and awareness staff, security people as relying heavily on, 33–34
Tribe of Hackers: Cybersecurity Advice from the Best Hackers in the World (Carey and Jin), 5
TTX (tabletop exercises), creation of to help management chain and leadership understand security, 248–249
Twitter
as learning option, 105
making connections via, 135
for placing job postings, 225
Two-year degree, as training option, 50

U

Underrepresented people. *See also* minority
promotions and career development for, 237–238
retaining diverse talent, 236–237

V

Verizon Data Breach Investigations Report, 88, 196, 290
Vulnerability management, as example of foundational element, 208
Vulnerability researcher, as red team job, 33

W

Watkins, Michael D. (author)
The First 90 Days, 181, 243, 288
Websites
BSides Conferences, 288
CISO Series podcast, 289
Cloud Security Alliance, 289
Cybersecurity Mindmaps, 289
Cyberseek.org, 289
The Cyber Canon, 289
The Cyber Ranch podcast, 289
The CyberWire podcast, 289
Daniel Meissler: How to Start an Infosec Career, 290
Hacker Valley Studio Podcast, 289
Hacking Training, 290
HackTheBox, 290
International Consortium of Minority Cybersecurity Professionals (ICMCP), 288
International Systems Security Association (ISSA), 288
ISACA, 289
(ISC)2, 288
Leslie Carhart: Starting an Infosec Career, 289
LinkedIn Learning, 290
NIST NICE Career Framework, 289

Websites (*Continued*)
  Pluralsight Training, 290
  resources, to help you make sense of security job classifications and skill requirements, 35
  Risky Business podcast, 289
  SANS Institute, 289
  Smashing Security podcast, 289
  value of personal one, 78
  Verizon Data Breach Investigations Report, 290
  Women in Cybersecurity (WiCyS), 288
What Got You Here Won't Get You There: How Successful People Become Even More Successful (Goldsmith), 151, 287
What Works: Gender Equality by Design (Bohnet), 288
Whylie, Phillip L. (author)
  The Pentester Blueprint: Starting a Career as an Ethical Hacker, 58, 287
Women in Cybersecurity (WiCyS), 124, 232, 288
Women in Technology groups, 127
Work experience (listing of on résumé), 72–73
Workforce Framework for Cybersecurity (NICE Framework) Work Roles table, 35. *See also* National Initiative for Cybersecurity Education (NICE) (US)
Working from home, option of as security professional, 98
Wyche, Keith (author)
  Good Is Not Enough: And Other Unwritten Rules for Minority Professionals, 288

Y

Young, Valerie (author)
  The Secret Thoughts of Successful Women: Why Capable People Suffer from Imposter Syndrome and How Thrive in Spite of It, 161–162, 288

Z

Zero-trust, 160, 190, 207, 243
Zero-trust networking, 98
Zinsser, William (author)
  On Writing Well, 288